THE
Process

A Proven Strategy for Creating Emotionally Healthy Leadership in Relationships, Business and in Life

Bill Hoffman

Outskirts Press, Inc.
http://www.outskirtspress.com

ISBN: 978-1-9772-2860-4

All Bible verses referenced are from the New International Version, (NIV), of the Bible unless otherwise noted.

Outskirts Press and the "OP" logo are trademarks belonging to Outskirts Press, Inc.

PRINTED IN THE UNITED STATES OF AMERICA

Table of Contents

Prologue

"Objects in mirror are more broken than they appear."

At the time when we met Bill Hoffman, many in our industry referred to us a "power couple". One that has it all together due to a growing, successful business that were able to develop while working together. We were very high functioning on the outside and it appeared to others that we were thriving. We were on sold out stages around the world collecting awards and speaking to thousands on success principles. However, when the curtains closed, the crowds dissipated and the spotlight was no longer on us, we were left with ourselves and our relationship was crumbling. The truth was, we were heading for a divorce.

They say that "the Roman Empire fell from within". We weren't working to live, we were living to work and it began to show in our marriage. As business partners, we were working like a well-oiled machine. But as life and marriage partners, we were dying on the vine. Having been disconnected from our authentic selves, we were blinded by the layers of emotional wounds and childhood scripts that we thought was normal and until we were triggered, we became exceptionally good at wearing our masks and sweeping things under the rug.

In comes Bill and The Process. As we took the deep dive into our root systems, we came face to face with our brokenness. We sought him out to help us become the archeologist of our lives, excavate our past hurts and begin the healing process. We learned the unforced rhythm of grace as we learned and chose forgiveness. We began to live wholeheartedly in our authentic states. We found peace, restoration, unity and purpose, but more importantly we learned to love each other because of our flaws not just in spite of them.

When you take off your mask, it gives others permission to do the same. The Process not only saved our marriage and transformed our lives, but it permeated the core of our leadership and therefore transformed the entire culture of our organization who have found true freedom. We thought we were doing FINE but we had no idea... Our advice to you? Trust The Process.

...and put your seatbelt on because it's going to be one wild and life changing ride!

Tony and Frances Pappalardo
Founders, Customize Your Life

1
Overview

THIS BOOK GIVES you a close look at a Process I have used successfully to help couples understand and harness the dynamics of what I call "leadership from home." Although most of the examples I will be sharing with you involve couples, anyone can benefit from the Process. Whether your status is single, married, in a relationship, or "it's complicated," the Process has something important to offer to you, because it is all about leadership from home.

Leadership from home is not what most people understand when they hear the word "leadership." The kind of leadership I'm talking about is not necessarily about setting and defending the agenda for a team meeting, or designing your product, or supporting your customers, or focusing your marketing message, or setting up your strategic plan—although the *failure* to exert leadership from home can sabotage your efforts at leadership in any or all of those areas, and indeed in any aspect of your work life in which you aspire to a leadership role.

By the same token, leadership from home is not necessarily going to be focused on you improving the quality of your one-on-one interactions outside of the workplace with family members, friends, and with new acquaintances—although the *failure* to exert leadership from home can and often does make effective communication with these people difficult or impossible.

Leadership from home starts with finding out who you are meant to be in your most intimate space—which for most of us means the space we share with our life partner—and then being that person. It is all about understanding yourself so you can then understand, and be more effective in, your relationships with others.

The Process that brings leadership from home into reality is one I've developed, and tested, over a long period of years. It inspires leadership from the inside out: It emphasizes leading at home and in your own life first, not second.

The Process is all about building a routine into your domestic life that supports lasting positive change in all your relationships, starting with your relationship with your partner.

The Process is not about learning workplace-related leadership principles and then "applying them" to your life. Instead, it is about being transformed into the kind of person who lives according to clear principles that support you, at every moment, in any and every environment.

What we will be examining here is relevant, and helpful, to anyone seeking to move from a position of stress and overwhelm to one of authenticity, potential, and personal fulfillment. I have found that its appeal is particularly powerful to couples—and specifically to couples who are working together on and in a business they own together. I wrote this book for them, but anyone can benefit from the principles we'll be examining here.

I find that, with such couples, at the outset of the relationship there is often a barely concealed sense of desperation, a sense that both the relationship and the business are in danger. The Process can give you the tool kit you need to understand, address, and reduce your level of vulnerability to that danger.

Here's what Laura had to say about how the Process helped her relationship:

> *Isolation used to be our "comfort zone." Andres and I used to let things pass and avoided addressing difficult situations. This kept us from each other . . . there was no oneness. The Process taught us to move past isolation. It taught us that follow-through, transparency, vulnerability, and selfless faith is what leads us to oneness. Every challenge continues to test us, but the foundation we are building now is stronger than ever, and it has helped us to persevere. Our relationship is no longer superficial. It is deep and connected. We have an entirely different point of reference now, one that has been worth every stretch.*

This Process that helped Laura and Andres—and hundreds of other working couples—must be experienced, not just read about. But reading about it, I have found, can be a good preparation for the experience. I decided to write about the Process for couples who haven't yet committed to it directly as part of an ongoing coaching relationship, so they could have a clearer sense of what the Process looks like and the extraordinary personal and professional results that it delivers.

This Process is a highly personal *internal* journey toward wisdom. It starts with you as an individual and is translated into every relationship you are part of, starting with your relationships at home.

If you decide to take this journey, your coach or mentor will challenge you to engage in a sustained Process of self-discovery over a long period. This journey will not happen overnight. It will follow certain specific, guided steps that support you as an individual. You will find transformation occurs over time as new patterns and tools are integrated and established in your life. This Process is, by definition, unique to each person who chooses to follow its steps. The importance of this kind of personal journey is rarely addressed, at least in my experience, when it comes to discussions about leadership development. To move from desperation to possibility we need a paradigm shift from "destination orientated" to "journey orientated." **We must be whole as individuals before we can exert leadership from home.**

Most of us have read or taken part in programs or "systems" that focus on the external characteristics of good, strong, capable, effective, or otherwise successful leaders. These programs, in my experience, usually prove challenging for those who try to put them into practice. Why? Because these externally oriented, tactical "leadership programs" fail to take into account the reality that true leadership always expresses itself from the inside out.

When there are business and executive failures, these usually arise not because a leader didn't know the right tactics, not because the person didn't know how to get the job done,

but rather because of an *internal* gap or disconnect of some kind. Most leadership "systems" simply ignore this fact.

We say that a leader who fails the team and the organization does not "walk his or her talk." What we mean is, **there's a lack of congruence between the inside of the person and the outside expression of leadership**. Time after time, we see that when there is a failure of leadership, there is this tension between what the person *says* he or she values, and what he or she *actually* values in practice as reflected in the world of action and choice. I call this the gap between values (that which we say guides us) and virtues (that which truly defines us to the outside world—namely our actions).

The kinds of leadership problems I am talking about may express themselves as greed, self-seeking, a lust for power, a willingness to manipulate, blame, persecute, or mislead others, and in any number of similar areas. These are, fundamentally, issues of morality. They are not instances of incomplete education or undeveloped talent in certain narrowly defined skill areas. They are signs of a deficit in the leader's emotional and spiritual health. They are signs that there is something missing inside.

I believe this disconnect between our stated values and our evident virtues is, fundamentally a moral problem—a disconnect between behaviors that support us as moral beings and behaviors that don't. Such moral disconnects carry—for me and for the people I coach, counsel, or mentor—a clear spiritual dimension.

I realize that the word "spiritual" is scary for some people. I will have a lot more to say about spirituality in subsequent chapters. For now, please understand you can benefit from the Process, and many people have, regardless of your religious beliefs and regardless of whether or not you believe in God. Consider this basic principle, which is our starting point:

It is literally impossible for us to grow in leadership capacity without growing internally, in terms of our own emotional and spiritual health, as experienced at home.

This is true not just in the world of business, but in our personal lives as well. In fact, all effective leadership begins in the home. Leadership is not something that can be pasted on externally. If our home life is in turmoil, we cannot and will not lead rightly in business, or anywhere else.

In this book, you'll learn the difference between mere "success" and true prosperity. You'll learn the difference between a life based on fixation on your to-do list, and a life rooted in a clear sense of purpose—a personal commitment to identify and live the life you were meant to live. You'll come to understand, at a deep, personal level, that we are all designed to be human *beings,* not human "doings." And you will, I believe, discover, in the Process, a remarkable new pathway into genuine and powerful living at home, in business, and in all your relationships, through the daily pursuit of emotional and spiritual growth and health.

Leadership is based in love, and love is expressed in relationships, not skill sets. Many failures in leadership, after all, are not tactical, but moral.

So, what *is* this Process? Is it about your saving your marriage? Is it about saving your business? Is it about discovering the "real" you, the "you" you were meant to be, designed to be?

The answer is yes. The Process is all about building a routine into your domestic life that supports lasting positive change in all your relationships, starting with your relationship with your partner.

Let's get started!

STUDY QUESTIONS

Consider keeping a journal or notebook to record your answers to these questions. Answer each question in as much detail as you can.

Can you think of any ways that "destination orientation"—the viewpoint that fixates on outcomes in a relationship rather than on process—has undermined your relationship? If so, how has it done that?

Are there any areas of your life where you have stated values, but not lived them? If so, what are those values?

What are some examples of leadership tactics you have learned and executed? Have these tactics supported your ability to be an effective leader in your spiritual or personal life? Why or why not?

How do you define prosperity? How do you define success?

2
Some Background

IT MAY BE easier to understand the Process we will be examining here if I share a little bit of my own story. This has helped serve as an introduction to the Process, I've learned, because my story and the story of the Process overlap.

I grew up in the suburbs of New Jersey in a severely dysfunctional family. My mother was an alcoholic, and my dad didn't know what to do about that. I couldn't wait to get out of the house. The first chance I got, I started running all over the country, trying to escape the pain and brokenness of my family situation.

I couldn't really find any place where I fit in. I kept bouncing back and forth between the East Coast and the West Coast, and each time I moved, I noticed my life was more of a mess. I became an alcoholic myself, and eventually I became a drug addict. I got a job as a bartender, which I guess made me a professional alcoholic. I lost track of time and place, and bad things started happening in rapid succession. I got a DWI in California. My dad died. I moved back out to

New Jersey for a while, and I picked up a DWI out there, too. Then my mom died.

I was all alone in the world, a fifteen-year-old in a thirty-year-old body, when I hit bottom and started going to AA meetings.

I finally got sober. I married a girl who was twelve years younger than I was. I wanted us to live the American dream. We got the house in the suburbs and we got the picket fence; the only thing we were missing was the two and a half kids. I had started my own business: I had an auto detailing shop working with Ferraris and Porsches in a ritzy area of Central New Jersey. So what if I was emotionally unavailable? Weren't most guys?

I hit bottom for the second time when my marriage failed and my business collapsed. In short order, I lost my business, lost my wife, got divorced, and to top it all off I had some bizarre health problem that nobody could make sense of. There was blood in my urine, and the doctors had no idea why. (They never did figure that one out.) I ended up alone again, working for the guy I had sold my business to. I was sick and severely depressed.

I surrendered my life to Christ because I didn't know what else to do. I knew I didn't want to start drinking again. But I also knew something major had to change in my world. I was home alone in my shop one night when I found myself thinking, "God, I just can't do this anymore. I just can't." And somehow, He saved me. He reached down and he pulled me out of that pit. I didn't know what was happening to me at the time. Nobody was standing there and witnessing to me. Nobody was saying, "You need to come to Jesus, brother." Nobody was there with me except God.

So I began going to church regularly, and God was working on my heart and planting a vision in me for doing things in this life other than just working and having a business. I wound up going on a retreat, and I heard about this ministry that was just starting up called New York City Relief. The ministry had dedicated a converted bus to work with the homeless in New York City.

I sold my house, which basically meant the bank got its money back, and I went to go work with this ministry, which was just starting up. I had no money, no insurance, no salary. I became an urban missionary. I was working in the ministry. And I was inspired, for the first time in my life, by the act of helping people. I found my life's calling and my purpose. I became a pastor in 1997.

About a year into my work with New York City Relief, I met Stephanie, an unemployed nurse who was also doing volunteer work for the homeless in New York City. We fell in love, and we got married. I had become a leader within the ministry by the time of our wedding . . . but the truth was I wasn't leading at home, and as a result, our marriage was headed for troubled waters.

I had divided my life into compartments; my marriage was a tiny little box I had set off from all the other things I was doing. My work was my life. The ministry was my life. I had carried my baggage and my inability to have a healthy relationship into my second marriage. **I was thinking, "Well, now I'm a Christian, now I'm a leader, and I'm OK. The marriage is OK. We have our problems now and then, but basically we're fine."**

There's an old saying that "fine," in this context, actually stands for fouled up, insecure, neurotic, and emotional—but I hadn't come across it yet.

We weren't fine. I was emotionally unavailable to my wife, and that was a major threat to our relationship. I had absolutely no idea of the height of the cliff I was pushing us toward. There is a saying in ministry work: "Don't mistake the blessing of God for his approval." At this stage of my life, I was mistaking those two things. I saw the gifts He had given me to support the ministry as a sign that He approved of the way I was showing up in my marriage.

This complacency of mine was a trap, a trap that many individuals and couples fall into. It was a danger zone I came in later years to learn is called the "tolerable recovery" zone. Within this zone, couples reach a place of settling, of tolerating each other, of choosing not to address the real issues, of making room for a familiar but sterile, empty place where there is no growth, no learning about each other, and no sense of oneness.

This place is there as long as people allow it to exist. It kills relationships. It can come to seem absolutely normal, which is how it seemed to me after a couple of years with my wife. I thought this was normal in marriage. I thought I could reach a place where we could coexist in a tolerable fashion, and if you argue with each other, that doesn't matter anyway, because everything will all go under the bridge, and not be dealt with in any effective way at all. But things don't go under the bridge. They get swept under the rug. And eventually you have to deal with them.

The tolerable recovery zone is a place of faithlessness, but not a place of hopelessness . . . yet. That hopelessness comes later. You see, this place of tolerating allows only so much time, but I treated it like it would last forever. I didn't realize it, but erosion was taking place. It's like the old parable about the frog in the pan of water on the stove. Put a frog in a pan of room temperature water on the stove, slowly turn up the heat, and it won't jump out. It gradually gets used to the temperature increase—until it boils to death.

My point here is that I was complacent, and complacency kills relationships.

When you go on like I was going on, particularly in marriage, you will boil to death. Hopelessness will set in, and disillusionment, and dissatisfaction, and these will lead to emptiness, and to crisis—even if you have fooled yourself into thinking that you're fine.

I really thought we were OK. I thought I was successful, and that because I was successful, any problem that came up would somehow work itself out. That seems monumentally self-absorbed to me now, but it was how I was thinking. I was succeeding at being in ministry. I was getting people off the streets and into more productive relationships. I was helping people put alcohol and drugs behind them. I was winning all kinds of accolades and winning all kinds of praise from all kinds of people. Why wouldn't problems solve themselves for me? But the reality was that I was working hard during the day and then coming home at the end of the day and giving nothing. I said I didn't believe in divorce. But my actions at home told a very different story.

My stated values were not lining up with my actions, so therefore my values were not my virtues at that point.

My work life and my home life were utterly separate. I wasn't leading from home.

And so it shouldn't have been a surprise to me when I came home one night and my wife looked me in the eye and told me that she wanted a divorce. But it was.

It was like a punch in the chest. I couldn't breathe. I thought, "Here I go again. History is repeating itself." I felt as lost as I had ever been. And I had felt very, very lost at earlier points in my life.

The moment my wife said those words to me, the moment I heard "I want a divorce," the moment I saw that I was staring at the possibility of not one but two failed marriages, I was shocked into a new phase of my life. I realized in that moment that I was screwed up and needed help. I needed to start over. Once Stephanie and I had received some intensive counseling, support, and guidance from some very patient, dedicated, and generous people, I was inspired. I started to think about a whole new structure, a whole new way of approaching our marriage, a whole new way of approaching *life*—a whole new Process.

The Process I developed as a result of my own certainty about having so disastrously sabotaged both of my marriages ended up rescuing a lot of other couples in crisis. Yet whenever people ask me why I am so certain that this Process works, I tell them the simple truth of my own experience: I know that it works because it worked for us. Stephanie and I have been married now for twenty-seven years. This book shows you how the Process saves marriages, and saves so much more, too.

A few more points are important to share here before we move on. **First, because this Process focuses on the individual first, it is not, and must not be confused with, "marriage counseling" or "couples' therapy."** Not only can you do the self-assessment and self-evaluation we will be discussing outside of the context of your domestic life, you *must* do it for yourself first if you expect it to yield meaningful positive results in your other relationships.

Second, **reading this book is not the Process.** It's an initial step in understanding the Process, which unfolds over time with the help of a coach or mentor. While the Process has indeed worked for hundreds of couples I've shared it with and coached, that doesn't mean it's the same thing as perfection. The goal here is progress, not perfection. My marriage isn't perfect; Stephanie and I are still a work in progress, as are all of the couples with whom I've worked over the years.

A big part of what the Process is all about is adopting the journey orientation I mentioned a little earlier, rather than a destination orientation. As human beings, we are always journeying. We never "arrive" and proceed with life without any further mix-ups or misunderstandings, functioning properly at long last. That's not how human life works, and thank goodness, because there would be no continued growth if that were the case. Healthy human beings are all about growth. We need trials of all kinds to help us to grow, mature, learn, and become closer to each other. Helping people understand those trials, helping them to identify and internalize the lessons lying hidden within them, is a big part of the coach or mentor's job. This is a job that results in an ongoing series of discoveries for all involved. It takes time and persistence. It must be done in person. It is not accomplished overnight. You can even argue that this job is never truly finished.

Third, and perhaps most importantly, **this is not a religious observance.** Although I am a Christian pastor and I will from time to time be sharing relevant Scripture passages with you, my goal is not to convert you to any particular set of spiritual practices or beliefs. For the purposes of our time together here, consider the possibility that I am not, for you, a religious man, but a practical man. The Process works because it gives you tools you can use to create positive results in your life and in your relationship, not because it is focused on religious dogma. If you come across concepts that sound religious to you, my strong advice to you is that you use what is useful and relevant to you and ignore what isn't. The Process is, above all else, pragmatic. You can be, too. For years now, I have been advising those who take part in the Process—many of whom are atheists and agnostics—to treat each seemingly "religious" concept like eating chicken wings. **Eat the meat . . . spit out the bones.**

STUDY QUESTIONS

FINE stands for Fouled Up, Insecure, Neurotic, and Emotional. When you say things are FINE in your relationship, does this definition ever apply? Why or why not?

Have you and your partner ever found yourselves living in tolerable recovery? If so, what is an example of an event or decision that makes you say that?

Are there any areas of your life where you have used external success to compensate for internal failures or shortcomings? If so, what are those areas?

Have you ever had a relationship event that felt like a punch in the chest? What was your response to that event?

How would you describe your spiritual belief system? How has it affected the choices you make? Give some examples.

3
Your True Self

CARL JUNG ONCE observed that "The privilege of a lifetime is to become who you truly are." This journey to one's true self is the key to a successful marriage, and the key to success in the various other relationships we forge as adults. But finding and expressing one's authentic self is, first and foremost, the critical task for married people, and as such it is the chief aim of the Process.

The authentic self is one that is not false or copied or improvised to suit the needs of the moment. It is the self that is present when no one is looking. It is genuine and real, expressing your true nature and beliefs. Living your authentic self means living from your center, living from the part of you that has been created for the purpose that is your life's plan. Most people do not live this way, which is why most marriages don't work.

It is a cliché to say that a good marriage requires authenticity. Strictly speaking, it's not accurate to say this. **What a working marriage really requires is two authentic selves that are authentically**

committed to each other. But in order to be authentically committed to someone else, we must first discover and be comfortable with our own authentic self. This requires being without artifice or subterfuge, and then doing what gives the most meaning to our life. Such being must not be confused with approval seeking or blame allocating, and such doing must not be confused with doing what is expedient or doing what is expected by others.

Building a successful marriage, then, means focusing on our own self first. This surprises some people, but it is true. In order to be a partner in a functioning marriage, you must first locate and support your true self. You must find a life that feeds your soul and gives you a sense of purpose and mission. It's being in touch with your Creator and specifically with your Creator's assignment of the value of who you are.

An authentic self operates energetically from a wellspring of unconditional love. When this love is fully active, a person feels interconnected, operates in integrity, and experiences peace, harmony, and understanding in all activities.

Authentic individuals are thus able to give to their partners, and receive from their partners, unconditional love. This is love that renews itself even in challenging situations and even in the face of seemingly intractable conflicts. This unconditional love allows both partners in the marriage over time to grow as people and to become who God created them to be, and then, in Divine order, to become one—even in the midst of challenging life situations.

This makes perfect sense. The one who has been forgiven much, loves much. But it is the _true_ self that must do the forgiving.

If you struggle with being your true self around your partner—or if you don't know who your true self is—your relationship is at risk. The Process, applied conscientiously over time with the guidance of a mentor, can dramatically lower that risk. **Most of the couples I work with have not, at the beginning of our time together, identified their true self or become comfortable sharing that self with their spouse.** They may experience the symptoms of that inauthenticity, and those symptoms may connect to significant problems within the relationship, but the realization that they have created a surface persona, a coping mechanism for interacting with their spouse, is usually not part of their conscious life. Like I did, they cope and hope. They find a way to convince themselves they are "fine," without acknowledging that what this really means is that they are fouled up, insecure, neurotic, and emotional.

As Brennan Manning put it, **"Living out of the false self creates a compulsive desire to present a perfect image to the public so that everybody will admire us and nobody will know us."**

TYLER AND MELANIE'S STORY

At the outset, I didn't really know that we even needed to seek guidance and help as a couple. All I knew was that I had started to notice patterns in my own life. There was a pattern of anger, and a pattern of a fear of rejection, and eventually I saw that these patterns led to conflicts and struggles that sometimes made the relationship extremely challenging. But still, somehow, for the longest time, to the outside world, and even to each other, I thought we were fine. At the outset, I was skeptical of working with a mentor. I understood that you get help from an accountant when you have an accounting problem, and that you get help from a lawyer when you have a legal problem, but I didn't have any sense that when you had problems with the most important thing in your life, your marriage, you go to someone to work on yourself. That just wasn't even on my radar screen. —Tyler

I moved here from Germany. Looking at my family, and at my own past history, I always thought that I had a great childhood, and that I had always been well protected. I was literally blocking out memories

to the contrary. I had no idea that they were there. Tyler and I had had a long-distance relationship. We spent one year together in the US, then I went back to Germany, then I came to live full time in the US. We spent about four years after that living together, but we really hadn't learned how to live together as a couple harmoniously.

We just didn't realize that that was a skill that needed to be mastered. We were fighting a lot, and I was going through a period of deep depression, but I tried to cover that up. Fortunately, we have a mentor who works with us on our business planning who picked up on what was going on. She sat me down and said, "Melanie—how are you doing, really? What's going on?" That was the first real discussion about where things were for me and how difficult things were in my marriage. I knew we loved each other, but deep down, I wasn't sure if that was enough. That mentor pointed us toward Bill, and that's how we came to work with him.

—Melanie

As it turned out, both Tyler and Melanie had complex personal histories involving personal trauma that were keeping them from expressing who they really were to each other. They each had developed a complex root system of assumptions, emotional responses, and defense mechanisms that prevented them from being able to accept their own choices and their own responsibility for what was going on in their lives—and in their marriage. This meant their partnership suffered, even as they told themselves (and the outside world) things were "just fine." Things were not just fine. They were growing apart, and emotional intimacy within the context of the relationship had grown increasingly difficult. So, they began working with me. I met with them as a couple in the first session, to get a sense of the communication dynamic within the marriage, and then (as is standard within the Process) I moved to working with each of them individually, using the one-on-one sessions to help each of them get a sense of what was standing in the way of expressing full responsibility for their own choices in life. This is not easy for most people, and it was not easy for Tyler or Melanie. But it was essential if they wanted to create a functional intimate and domestic life, and that was something they were both committed to doing.

Melanie's case was particularly challenging. It emerged, during our work together, that she had for many years repressed memories of serious childhood sexual abuse. This meant that both she and Tyler had been "flying blind" for their entire marriage about root causes of many of Melanie's obstacles when it came to physical and emotional intimacy! Only through working the Process—and in Melanie's case seeking the help of a qualified therapist who could help her to understand and come to terms with what had happened to her—were they each able to reach a point of self-acceptance that made acceptance of each other, and effective communication within their marriage, possible. Reaching that point took a lot of time, effort, and commitment, but they each knew the alternative was the collapse of intimacy within their relationship. And so they kept working the Process I shared with them, because they were certain they would be unable to avoid that collapse on their own.

Melanie told me in no uncertain terms that, without the Process, she would have given up on her marriage and gone back to Germany. Thankfully, that did not happen. Now that they have each established personal leadership of their own lives, they have each uncovered their true self and each committed fully to the marriage, which is now thriving and the center of each of their lives. Today, they are committed partners in business—and in life. They credit the Process with having gotten them to that point by enabling them to uncover and then fully commit their true, authentic selves to their marriage.

The Process by which you, too, can uncover your true self, and commit that true self to your own fullest potential, unfolds in the following steps, each of which is the focus of a chapter in this book:

- Temperament
- Self-awareness and journaling
- Forgiveness/releasing of judgment
- Taking thoughts captive (engaging)
- Effecting inner healing
- Maintaining newfound disciplines

STUDY QUESTIONS

In what ways do you create a false or inauthentic self?

What assumptions, emotional responses, and defense mechanisms prevent you from being genuine and authentic?

Are there any events in your past that may be preventing you from being open, authentic, and transparent with your partner? If so, what are they?

In what ways do you and your partner "cope and hope"?

On its own, is love enough to address or resolve dysfunctional behavior patterns in your relationship? Why or why not?

4
Temperament

TEMPERAMENT IS YOUR God-given nature, your inborn traits, and the way you relate to those around you.

Evaluating your temperament is the first step of the Process, the step without which progress in the other six steps is literally impossible. This evaluation is conducted, not by means of any subjective personal analysis that relies on the impressions or prejudices of your mentor, but on a highly reliable assessment of likely personal traits and social predispositions generated by the Arno Profile System. This is a life-changing tool I'll refer to from here on out simply as the assessment. The assessment is a clinical diagnostic tool developed by Drs. Richard and Phyllis Arno, the founders of the National Christian Counselors Association. It is used to assess a person's God-given temperament. My experience, and the experience of hundreds of clients, is that it is invaluable in helping individuals get a better understanding of themselves and of their spouse. It also helps the mentor working with them very quickly get "up to speed" regarding the likely problems and challenges in the relationship.

The assessment delivers results that are startlingly accurate—so much so that couples often share astonishment and disbelief at the mentor's ability to use it to summarize the major challenges in both their private lives and their work lives, even though they have revealed nothing about these challenges in face-to-face discussions. Yet for all its prescience, the assessment requires no huge investment in the time or patience of the person whose temperament is being assessed. All it requires is honesty, and the willingness to invest perhaps a quarter of an hour's focused attention on a series of test-like questions. These sessions are typically conducted in private, and at the individual's convenience, on one's phone or personal computer. For best results, I recommend you conduct the assessment without interruption.

When properly administered, the assessment more or less instantly reveals the "hidden problems" that might normally take a mentor seven or eight one-on-one sessions to identify. Assume these sessions are taking place once a week, and you can see how the use of the assessment can jump-start the Process by giving the partners, as well as the mentor, a two-month head start when it comes to understanding the major challenge areas in one's relationship with one's spouse and with the larger world.

What the assessment really does is allow us each to see who our Creator designed us to be. Once we have a clear sense of who that is, we can gain a better understanding of who we have become through learned behavior. We gain a better understanding of our own character—which can be, and often is, entirely different from what is presented to the outside world. If we are to learn who we really are, if we are to identify in our marriage and in all other areas of our life the best ways to express our true self, rather than the person we have learned to be (the masked self), we must closely examine our own temperament and the temperament of our life partner.

Look closely at the graphic below:

Building Blocks

THE MASK
Self-Selected "Personality"

The Mask is how we portray ourselves to the
world and in public; how we present ourselves.
The mask we wear is not who we really are.

CHARACTER
Man/Environment

Character is our adopted belief systems and learned
behaviors. Our character is developed within us by the
influences outside of us: Moral & religious belief systems,
upbringing, etc.

TEMPERAMENT
God-Given

Temperament is your God-given nature, your inborn traits and the
way you relate to those around you.

The Mask

Self-selected "personality"

The mask is how we portray ourselves to the
world and in public, how we present ourselves.
The mask we wear is not who we really are.

Character

Man/environment

Character is our adopted belief systems and learned

behaviors. Our character is developed within us by the influences outside of us: moral and religious belief systems, upbringing, etc.

Temperament

God-given

Our God-given nature, inborn traits, and the way we relate to those around us.

Notice that temperament is the bottom layer. It is who God made us to be, before environmental factors and our self-selected personality choices kicked in. This is what the assessment reveals: The self at the foundational level.

To isolate temperament, the foundation of who we really are, the assessment looks at our expressions and our needs in three different areas:

- Inclusion: our social orientation and intellectual energies
- Control: our willingness to make decisions and to accept responsibility for self-and/or others
- Affection: our need to express and receive love, affection and approval; our need for deep personal relationships

In each assessment, the following terms are used to identify the five basic temperaments[1] that can operate within those three realms:

I   *Four of these basic temperaments—Melancholy, Sanguine, Choleric, and Supine—may be designated in some cases as "compulsive," a scary-sounding word that simply means the person being assessed demonstrates a higher-than-average intensity of the characteristics of that temperament. If you happen to get a "compulsive" score, that's nothing to worry about. It just means the temperament in question is very strongly pronounced in your case.

- **Melancholy temperament:** characterized by a desire to be alone—independent, realistic, artistic, and creative
- **Sanguine temperament:** characterized by a need for people—bright and cheerful, with a sunny disposition
- **Choleric temperament:** characterized by a need to dominate and control situations, self, and others—often there is strong leadership potential here
- **Phlegmatic temperament:** characterized by low energy, an easygoing manner, and peacemaking abilities
- **Supine temperament**: characterized by indirect behaviors, a gentle spirit, and an inability to initiate; "a people pleaser" who lives to serve others

Each assessment is divided into the three categories of inclusion, control, and affection. Within each of these categories, one or more of these temperaments may be in play.

Here is why temperament is important: By honestly, fearlessly, and truthfully charting where your God-given nature operates most of the time in terms of inclusion, control, and affection, you can see where your own strengths and weaknesses are, where you need to focus your attention, and where you have already done work in your life. Not only that, but you can understand your partner at the same level of honesty, fearlessness, and truth—and with practice, gain a deeper understanding of why you and your partner need what you each need and behave as you each behave.

With a deeper insight on each other's temperaments, you can stop taking things personally.

It was like having a mirror held up to my face. What came back on the assessment was really who I was. After my assessment, it became much clearer to me not only what I was doing and why I was doing it, but what Tyler was doing and why he was doing that. It was just a very

deep and intimate portrait of our deepest motivations. It was quite powerful. —Melanie

Everything changed with the assessment. When you start answering these questions, you start really thinking deeply about what it was like to grow up in the environment you grew up in. For me, that was a first. Then, evaluating the results and discussing them with Bill, it was just remarkable to see how accurate it was and the kind of progress that you could make, very quickly, once you understood why you do what you do and why your partner does what they do. It was like your eyes were opened and you could see things that you had been overlooking for a very long time. By knowing your own temperament, by getting a fix on how you approach things and who you really are, you begin to get a much clearer understanding of where the real challenges in the relationship are going to come up. —Tyler

During my early discussions with couples, I'll make the point that conducting the assessment is an extremely important—and indeed nonnegotiable—early step on the journey because it helps *each* partner see how he or she is personally responsible for the brokenness that exists in the relationship.

In other words, there is no good guy and there is no bad guy. Both parties have gotten the relationship to the place where it is right now. Both must gain a deeper understanding of how the relationship has reached this point, and specifically of what personal traits and unfulfilled needs have been causing a disconnect. The time for winning an argument about who is at fault is over. The time for understanding ourselves and each other has come. The assessment makes that possible.

I also point out that our discussions about the results of the assessment will begin to make this reality clear, and that the reality will become clearer and clearer as the Process continues. Although the couples are sometimes skeptical about this, they will usually buy into what I am saying and agree to keep working the Process. Often, this is because they can tell, even in the very early going, that my familiarity with their assessment results has given me some important insights into who they really are as people, and what specific challenges they face.

Let's consider Tyler and Melanie as an example. I could tell even before we went into the detailed results of their assessments that there were certain structural issues connected to temperament that were likely to lead to patterns of conflict. Tyler's results indicated he was Sanguine in terms of inclusion, Melancholy compulsive in terms of control, and Sanguine compulsive in terms of affection. I don't expect those designations to mean a lot to you now, so I will just break them down for you: His assessment indicated that, temperamentally, at a fundamental level, Tyler was very social and he needed a lot of love, affection, and approval in his close relationships. And he was, at the same time, highly independent in other areas of his life.

So right way I knew Tyler needs a lot of love, and that he's likely to respond to the lack of love by walling himself off from his partner. Looking at Melanie's assessment I saw Melancholy in terms of control, Melancholy in terms of inclusion, and Phlegmatic in terms of affection. Translation: She's probably not very good in the affection department. Also, I know that she too, is highly independent. So right at the beginning, I knew there was a very good likelihood that there was a lack of emotional and physical intimacy between these two people, just based on their differences in temperament, and that this distance was likely to be deeply troubling for Tyler.

I said as much very early in our discussions, before they had told me anything of consequence about what was going on in their relationship. They looked at me as though I had somehow gotten access to a crystal ball that told me what was happening in their lives.

All I was really doing was identifying some of the likely challenges based on each of their temperaments.

And by the way, those early insights were not taking into account any brokenness that may have resulted from traumas or difficulties experienced in their early lives (which turned out to be a significant factor for both of them), or brokenness arising from their choices within adult relationships.

YOU MUST UNDERSTAND YOUR OWN TEMPERAMENT AND YOUR PARTNER'S TEMPERAMENT

Let me put it bluntly: **Understanding your own temperament and the temperament of your partner is a critical factor in the success or failure of your relationship.** Failing to gain this understanding typically leads to deep dysfunction. If you are serious about making your marriage the foundation of your life, if you are serious about leading from home, you will want to take the time to complete the assessment and then debrief with your mentor about its results.

In this chapter, I've sketched out the broad outlines of how the assessment works, and what the discussions that follow it typically sound like. But the complexities of each individual couple and the ways in which their assumptions and reactions are likely to present challenges go so much deeper than what I've laid out here that I can only urge you to take the next step by reaching out to a mentor—and the sooner the better. Consider what you've read here to be the equivalent of learning the names and the legal moves of the various pieces on the chessboard.

Consider gaining a practical understanding of your own temperament and its effect on your partner, and your partner's temperament and its effect on you, to be the equivalent of playing a game of chess with an experienced player. You've gotten a start here. Now it's up to you to take your game to the next level—the level of experience, rather than theory.

Keep in mind that whenever I examine and talk about my own temperament, I am actually examining and talking about "The Real Me." I am getting a clearer fix on why I do the things that I do, what the consequences of those actions of mine are on myself and others, and what my best path in life really is, based on who I really am.

I worked with one woman who had spent many years being a teacher, because her family had urged her to become a teacher. After her assessment, she realized the big reason that she had struggled for years to find happiness within that job was she was constitutionally averse to standing up in front of people and making speeches and presentations. This wasn't any shortcoming on her side. It was simply "The Real Her." Once she got a clear sense, through understanding of her own temperament, of who God had created when He created her, she was able to move past irrelevant factors like trying to please others and make choices that truly suited her as a person. She made a career transition to one-on-one counseling, and has been happy and fulfilled in that role. She was trying to please her earthly father, but was miserable in the reality of that. She became much happier when she set her sights on trying to please her heavenly Father.

We can't expect to identify our life's true purpose until we understand and come to terms with "The Real Me"—the good, the bad, and the ugly. And *until* we identify our true selves and the purposes that aligns with them best, we will struggle with our own brokenness.

In the Bible, the Apostle Paul wrestles with this very challenge. He had to come to terms with "The Real Me," just as all of us do. Paul was likely a Choleric; I say that because we know Paul was a murderer before he was struck blind by God so that God could turn him around. (A lot of Cholerics need that kind of dramatic intervention before they can truly "see" the impact of their behavior. They need a big event in their life to make them stop and re-evaluate.) When Paul came out of that blindness he had a vision of Jesus, and he gained a new set of challenges based on the inescapable reality of his own "Real Me." In the seventh chapter of the Epistle to the Romans, Paul writes, with painful honesty: *"I do not understand what I do" (Romans 7:15).*

This will sound very familiar indeed to anyone who has wondered how the negative attributes and patterns of action of his or her temperament seem to rise to the surface much more rapidly and more consequentially than the positive attributes. This "accentuation of the negative" is a symptom of not having come to terms with your own brokenness. Getting a clear picture of "The Real Me" is the first—and nonnegotiable—step toward understanding what you do and why you do it. Once you understand that much you will be in a position to gain a clearer understanding of what your true purpose in life ought to be.

Later, Paul concludes: *"Those who live according to the flesh have their minds set on what the flesh desires; but those who live in accordance with the Spirit have their minds set on what the Spirit desires" (Romans 8:5).*

For "flesh," read "brokenness." For "Spirit," read "God's guiding purpose for you."

Elsewhere in the Bible, in the first chapter of James, there is a potent metaphor involving a mirror: *"Anyone who listens to the word but does not do what it says is like someone who looks at his face in a mirror—and, after looking at himself, goes away and immediately forgets what he looks like. But whoever looks intently into the perfect law that gives freedom, and continues in it—not forgetting what they have heard, but doing it—they will be blessed in what they do" (James 1:23–24).*

Think of temperament as your chance to look at yourself clearly in the mirror, remember who you are, and then *act* on what you have learned about yourself.

STUDY QUESTIONS

Have you had your assessment done? If so, what have you learned about yourself and your partner, and about areas that need attention in your relationship?

If not, what are the obstacles standing in the way of you having the assessment done?

Are there any areas of your life where you do things, but don't know why you do them? If so, what are they?

5
Self-Awareness and Journaling

I USED TO call the second step of the Process journaling . . . but now I call it self-awareness and journaling. The new name, which emerged as a result of work I had done with many couples, reflects an important change in emphasis. This label more accurately describes what *always* has to happen before either partner can move on to the next step of the Process—forgiveness. There must be self-awareness, reflected in personal journaling that commits the perspective of that self-awareness to the written word.

Here in the second step of the Process there is a sustained personal effort on the part of each partner to dig deep down and reveal the true causes of their own deepest pain and their own most stubborn, recurrent struggles—and share all of that with each other. This work is not easy, and it does not happen overnight, but the simple reality is you can't move forward to forgiveness in your life without it. Of course, you can make any number of sounds with your mouth at any time, including the words "I forgive you," but the actuality of forgiveness will not take place in your life without this second step.

The fifth chapter of the epistle of James says, "Confess your sins to one another and pray for one another so you can be healed" (James 5:16). That's really the second step in a nutshell—once you get past the word "sins," which is in my experience a word that can stop a lot of people cold.

When James talks about us confessing our "sins" to one another, what he means, I believe, is we should confess our *brokenness* to one another. He means we should directly discuss the dysfunctional parts of our lives with the people we trust most, and then reach out for support in healing that brokenness.

In the framework of a couple working their way through the Process, "confession" simply means each partner talking honestly and fearlessly their personal "stuff" out loud, under the guidance of the mentor, and then writing about it. All of that takes practice.

The writing is an important part, because it enables people to revisit and re-experience important past events and relationships in a way that brings understanding and closure. Yet my experience is that journaling comes easily for some people, and not so easily for others. (temperament has a lot to do with this.) Inevitably, though, regardless of whether one initially feels comfortable with journaling or uncomfortable with it, the writing that brings closure is always preceded by a series of honest, open discussions that begin with the goal of isolating the specific unhealthy beliefs each partner holds—the beliefs that are to a greater or lesser degree undermining, not only the marriage, but all of their relationships. Such unhealthy beliefs include (but are certainly not limited to) beliefs about:

- Rejection: the belief that one simply does not belong
- Conditional self-esteem: the belief that "doing" is necessary to achieve self-worth, value, and/or recognition
- Control: the belief that control of people and/or situations is necessary in order to avoid pain

Other broad categories of unhealthy belief could include beliefs about one's own personality traits or one's perceived physical obstacles; one's status as a victim; one's right (or duty!) to retaliate in the face of conflict, hurt, or disagreement; and even one's very identity as a human being. Here is a hard truth: There are dozens of unhealthy belief systems we can fall into, and there are countless personal variations within those systems we can deploy to create and maintain deeply imbedded, highly dysfunctional, and highly personalized belief systems about ourselves and the world around us.

"As a man believes in his heart, so he is" (Proverbs 23:7).

Unhealthy beliefs trick us into believing that what we have trained ourselves, over a long period of years, is reality. One example of such a disempowering belief system would be the underlying belief "I am not worth loving." Another would be the underlying belief: "The people I love and trust always let me down in the end." We may not say these unhealthy, deeply held beliefs out loud, but whether we do or not, the sad truth is we build our lives around them.

The point of the self-awareness and journaling step is to identify and express disempowering beliefs— and, just as important, to identify and express the specific experiences that gave rise to them.

This means taking part in a deep series of ongoing discussions, led by the mentor, that help each partner isolate the specific events in their past history that had an influence in bringing about unhealthy beliefs . . . and their associated patterns of action and behavior.

Why do this? Why "dig up the past"? Because these predictable patterns of action and behavior so often create total BROKENNESS—not just with the partner, but with the world at large. And if we don't understand these patterns, we revert to what I call tolerable recovery: coping and hoping, with a side order of denial. Meanwhile, while we congratulate ourselves for "staying together for the kids" (or whatever other story we've come up with), our marriage continues to disintegrate—even if we do manage to distract ourselves from that daily disaster, temporarily, by earning more money, buying a bigger house, or having an affair.

Let me be very frank with you about something. Most people are not eager to do the work step two demands of them, work that, inevitably requires a closer, more sustained look at their childhood and their personal history than they are used to taking. Yet self-awareness is impossible without it . . . and a marriage in crisis or approaching crisis is almost certainly doomed *unless* this work is done.

Most of us are in deep ignorance about the past history, the belief systems, and the old assumptions that guide our actions. We don't even think these things have a significant impact on our behavior. But they do. Taken together, I call these influences our root system. If we don't make changes in the root system, then whatever surface changes we make, whatever weeds we think we've pulled out, won't make any difference. The same stuff will grow back, because the root system remains the same.

ROOT CAUSE ANALYTICS

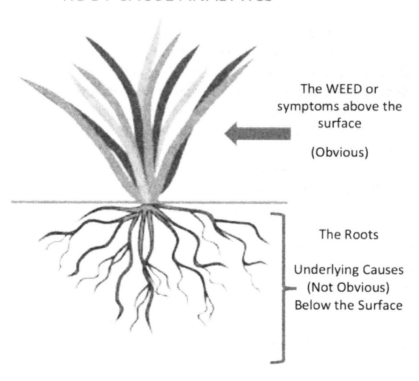

The WEED or symptoms above the surface

(Obvious)

The Roots

Underlying Causes
(Not Obvious)
Below the Surface

Clearing out your root system is not easy. I can clearly recall a conversation with one woman who had, separately from her husband, been having sessions with me for several weeks. I'll call her Rose. I looked Rose in the eye and said, "You know, Rose, based on the beliefs we've uncovered, and the impact those beliefs and their behaviors are having on your marriage, I think I should tell you directly that you have a lot of work to do if you want to turn this around."

Rose nodded and said, "I know I do, Bill."

"And?"

After a pause, she looked right at me and said, "And I think I don't feel like doing that work."

"Even if that means losing your marriage?"

"Yes. Even if that means losing my marriage."

I've heard dozens, probably hundreds of people say essentially the same thing when they reach the second step. They push back. But what they're really saying is they don't want to be accountable for understanding their own root system. That's a mistake.

I always tell people, **"You are as sick as your secrets."** The stuff that is still inside them, unexplored, the stuff that they have not had the courage to talk about, is inevitably what will show up as problems in their marriage—and everywhere else.

Sometimes couples come to me asking for help in changing specific bad behaviors. One or both partners in a marriage may understand they've made bad choices on many levels, and they are usually sincere in their desire to acknowledge those choices and become an all-around better person. As part of their assessment, they are exposed to their temperaments, and they quickly come to see both the weaknesses and strengths of their temperaments. Typically, this is followed by a strong desire to "change"—to start "doing things differently" and bring about the change they are looking for in their life and in their marriage. The problem is, if they could "do" the right things in the first place, they would have likely done so already! The real problem is more deeply imbedded. We have to dig below the surface . . . and look at the root system.

When we have toxic roots—developmental trauma, addictions, experiences of childhood of rejection, you name it—we will produce toxic weeds on the surface. This will cause our temperament traits to be manifested on the weakness end of the spectrum! We will incur difficulties in our relationships on virtually every level. Insecurities, fears, inhibitions, pride, self-delusion—all these things are deeply rooted. They are symptoms of deeper problems. Those problems cannot be fixed by simply *wanting* transformation. We tend to be destination oriented; we think to ourselves, "I want to just fix this and move on," as if everything beyond the point of that "fixing" will somehow be perfect from that point forward. It's quite common for someone dealing with problems in their marriage to say to me, "Look, I just want to get on with my life"—meaning they want to circumvent the work necessary to identify and deal with the root causes of their problems. I often reply, "What exactly are you getting on *with?*"

We must set out to uproot these problems in our history by doing a deep dive. We have to dig deep down through all the layers of our personal history. We have to fearlessly examine our own personal archeology, if you will. If we don't, we may achieve temporary change in behaviors, but that change won't last. In order for the change to last, the roots need to be changed. We must uproot the painful, underlying causes and plant new seeds in their place that will grow into good fruit. Self-awareness and journaling are what bring about a change in the root system.

I often use the example of someone trying to get rid of the weeds by mowing the lawn. All this will do is bring the weeds to the same length of the grass—and by tomorrow morning the weeds will be poking out above the grass. **It is the deep roots that keep the weeds strong. We have to dig the weeds out by the roots if we want to get rid of them!**

WEEDING TAKES TIME

The "weeding" step of journaling and self-awareness is usually an extended one. No matter how long it takes, it must always precede the next step in the process, forgiveness/releasing of judgment. Meaningful forgiveness is impossible without a clear understanding of your own root system, and journaling and self-awareness is where that work happens. It is unheard of for that kind of work to happen overnight, although that is what many people I work with initially expect.

Often, we get so used to "making things happen" in the realm of professional achievement that we expect important events in our personal lives to unfold on a similarly aggressive schedule. The second step of the Process doesn't work like that. We pull out weeds at the rate we pull out weeds. If we manage to extract the whole root, getting rid of the weeds happens at a faster rate than if we just trim the leaves. But we can't simply order the weeds to vanish. We have to locate them, get a hold on them, and pull them out ourselves by allowing God access to them through forgiveness and releasing of judgments. That's not the mentor's job. It's our job. And it happens at the speed at which it happens, which is up to us.

This is why I tell couples to be patient, to work the Process, and to keep an open mind about where the examination of each partner's root system is taking them. When they tell me they're eager to see "results" or to "move on with their lives," I tell them to take the energy they're expending on wishing the Process were proceeding faster and use it to focus on the reality of their own family history and its impact on their adult lives.

We each reach our "moments of truth" with regard to our own Root System at our own pace. That is just the way it is. It took Sara more than a year of guided discussion, journaling, and self-assessment to reach the point where she could write this:

> *Shock is what I felt when I found out why I've done what I've done. Before discovering my temperament and*

before getting to the root of the issue, I had no clue that I was operating out of grief. But I was.

I didn't like to get too close to people. I didn't like to reveal too much of myself. Why? Because I was afraid, deep down, of being rejected, or even worse, abandoned. Although I was never physically abandoned by my parents, I experienced emotional abandonment from my father at a very young age and later as an adolescent. He had a major drinking problem.

I decided early on that he didn't understand my needs or wants. How could he, if he couldn't understand that I just really wanted him to stop drinking? I remember I would wait up for him late nights and pray that nothing happened to him. I would pretend I was asleep so that I wouldn't get my mom upset.

I was always worried about him when he would go out drinking. One night he was out late, and I was more worried than usual, and I think I might have called him fifty times and no answer. He finally called me back—but instead of telling me he was sorry for not picking up the phone, he yelled at me for calling him so many times in a row. He said that many calls in a row are meant for emergencies only and that I should know that he was OK. I was eleven years old. I had been worried about him and all I had gotten in return was anger. It was a horrible experience.

Fast-forward to 2017. My boyfriend at the time, Eric, goes missing two hours before a party that we'd been planning for months to attend. He too was an addict and he too was emotionally unavailable. Deja vu: I called him multiple times and got no answer. Playing out the same drama all over again.

It wasn't until that relationship ended that I became desperate for answers. On the outside I appeared happy, fun, and secure, but on the inside I was broken, clinging to whatever man showed me attention. That relationship exposed my deepest insecurities: the fear of being rejected, abandoned, humiliated, and misunderstood. I took on that relationship as a project. I thought I could prove my worth by changing him. Except the joke was on me.

I was eventually confronted with what was really happening in both of those situations: a little girl yearning for her father's love.

I had buried this part of me so deep inside of me that it took a full year for me to be able to sit down and write this.

I was so ashamed of myself. I didn't know I was grieving; didn't know how badly I was hurting due to my inability to experience love from my father.

I always thought of my father as the provider of the household, yet I didn't feel loved or seen. I felt so much anger toward my father that I dated men who were exactly like him, to try to make them love me as he should have loved me. And believe it or not, I even found a way to make myself feel guilty about that. I felt as if I was ungrateful because there are so many people out there who wish they had a dad.

I kept on coming up with excuses for Eric, such as he came from a hard childhood, or that he too was never shown love and that's why he didn't know how to give it to me. He left his home country and came to the US at young age and basically has been in survival mode ever since. I even made excuses for his drinking and how it was my fault that it affected me so much because it wasn't as "bad" as I've seen others deal with. I was repressing huge amounts of anger. Anger was something I've always felt as bad and unnecessary but experiencing it has helped me so much in this process. I felt anger that my dad's inability to love me has kept me away from experiencing real love from others, anger that because of my childhood I'm insecure and needy. But it was only after accepting anger that I found the strength to write this letter. Being angry made me realize that I really hadn't forgiven my father, even though I thought I had, and that I was still operating out my weaknesses.

Digging deep has lifted this giant weight off my shoulders so that I can now begin to accept myself and love myself a little bit more each day. My coach Pastor Bill told me I had to allow myself to hate what my father did, and not just make appeasements toward him, before I could genuinely forgive him. That sounded crazy, but it worked. Once I expressed that emotion our communication improved. My father now knows how to hug me because I was finally able to tell him how I want to be hugged. To many this may seem minuscule, but to me this is life changing. I know I have a long way to go in this journey but what I am certain is that my brokenness is God's gift to me so that I can truly become who He intended me to be.

JOURNALING MEANS RELIVING THE KEY EXPERIENCES

Let me emphasize: There is no breakthrough worthy of the name, either in our marriages or in any other facet of our lives, without the experience of deep, reflective self-assessment followed by the parallel experience of writing about what has actually happened in our lives. The act of writing may take us a while to feel comfortable, but it needs to happen eventually because only journaling in this way allows us to relive on an emotional level what has happened to us, process those events, and express any emotions that need to be expressed—emotions that may have been suppressed for years or even decades. This is often a painful experience. But the next step of the process cannot happen without it.

Sometimes the act of journaling transitions into the beginnings of forgiveness of self and others. Here is an example of a journaling entry that does just that.

I FORGIVE YOU

This may be the hardest exercise I've ever had to do. I don't think I've ever thought of the possibility of forgiving myself before.

Ever since you were just a little girl, Esther, maybe four years old, your biggest longing was to be a wife and a mother. You lived focused on finding your Prince Charming. You were always in love with someone.

I forgive you, Me, for seeking love in the wrong places from an early age. I forgive you, Me, for the lies you told everyone around you out of fear, and for the lies you told to get away with something, or because you were angry, or for whatever reason it may have been.

I forgive you for having fallen in love with a man you shouldn't have, and for doing your best to make him notice your presence. I forgive you for having "boyfriends" during those years you were in love with him, only to try to forget him. I forgive you for hurting the hearts of those kids who were crazy about you. I forgive you for giving your virginity to that man at just eighteen years old and for having been silent when he later raped you, for fear of being punished or judged. I forgive you for deciding to keep everything inside.

I forgive you for lying to your mom so many times, for running away from home at night so men could come looking for you. I forgive you for not respecting you or respecting your body. I forgive you for showing one personality to people, especially your family and the people of the church, and then being a totally different person behind their back. I forgive you for all the damage you caused yourself by living that empty, meaningless life. I forgive you for the adulterous relationship you had at twenty-one with a married man, a man forty years older than you. I forgive you for keeping that up for two years. I forgive you for your naivete, for your ignorance, for all the things you did even knowing they were not good things to do. I forgive you for knowing they were sinful and doing them anyway to please the desires of your flesh. I forgive you for all the married men you wrote to even though you knew they were married. And I forgive you for all the sinful acts you committed in your mind, wishing that one day they would become a reality.

I forgive you for judging your dad by the life he has led, for the times you have spoken ill of him and thought ill of him. I forgive you for the times you've spoken ill of your mom. I forgive you for the times you've offended them both with your actions and words.

I forgive you for speaking ill of your sister and your brother and judging their choices in the life they have decided to live.

I forgive you for the times you haven't been a good wife. I forgive you for ignoring many times how privileged you are to have Esteban as your husband, lover, best friend, and confidant. I forgive you for the times you haven't valued all that he does for you.

I forgive you for the times you have been a bad wife, mother, daughter, sister, friend, and citizen. I forgive you for all the times you have not behaved like the Christian you know you are.

I forgive you for all the times that you feel that you are not enough, for all the times that you feel you are not worthy to receive love and that you are not worthy to receive forgiveness. I forgive you for all the times you compare yourself to other people and think less about yourself. I forgive you for the times you haven't kept your word and for the times your YES hasn't been YES.

You're not perfect, Esther, and you'll probably continue to fail in many things, but remember to have grace with yourself and create a habit of forgiving yourself, of loving yourself as you are, of accepting yourself as you are and seeing the beautiful qualities that God has bestowed upon you. Focus on that. I forgive you, Me, for all the evil and harm you have done, for all the things you're not proud of and have remorse for.

Everything is left behind—you're free.

Esther continued her journaling, eventually using writing as a tool for forgiving all the men who had abused her, for forgiving her mother and father for not assigning value to her because they wanted a boy after a miscarriage, for forgiving her husband for problems he had brought into their relationship, and much more. Esther's was a special case because she happened to be simultaneously forgiving all of the people that had hurt and abandoned her in her life. This was her initial step into freedom—the freedom to accept herself and be who she genuinely is, the freedom to love and be loved genuinely, not only in her marriage but in other relationships.

A key moment in this transition came when Esther told me that, for the first time in her life, she had allowed herself to realize that she was angry and to express that emotion of anger. Prior to that, in talking about her past, she had always said she was hurt, not angry. Self-assessment and journaling allowed her to reach a point where she was free to allow herself to be angry and to hate what had been done to her. Once she reached that point, she stopped being a victim, forgave, and was free. We will be talking much more about forgiveness in the next chapter. What I want you to notice now, however, is that **self-assessment and journaling broke up the logjam and allowed the later step of forgiveness and releasing of judgment to occur**—and in Esther's case it occurred in a rush.

THE QUESTION OF TEMPERAMENT

The way you instinctively approach the vitally important second step of the Process is likely to depend heavily on your temperament.

Both Sarah and Esther were Supines. They're the ones who "layer down" their emotions. They are typically resistant to the deep dive necessary to experience and express the emotions connected with past experiences, and they will come up with elaborate narratives to avoid doing so. Very often, this pushback goes on for a lifetime and keeps true forgiveness from ever taking place. Fortunately, some Supines (like Sarah and Esther) respond, over time, to the coaching of a mentor.

The independent-minded Cholerics are often profoundly resistant to the whole complex of behaviors associated with self-assessment, journaling, and forgiveness. They are experts at justifying themselves. "So-and-so happened to me, yes, and what that means is that I am absolutely right in what I am doing now." Without coaching, they often miss the step where they acknowledge that their behaviors do in fact have an impact on others, and it may take them a while to accept the importance of examining the root causes of those behaviors.

Melancholy people are also highly independent. Melancholy people think and believe that they're right, and has ample evidence to support this contention. (The Choleric , by contrast, *knows* that they're right.) The big problem the Melancholy person faces is that they think all the time. They're like lawyers: They create intricate logical defenses of past behaviors and current ways of approaching issues. Usually, this mindset is devoted to creating and reinforcing personal defenses. However, when a mentor presents them with solid, unimpeachable reasons why resisting self-assessment is not working or is too expensive (for instance, when it becomes impossible to deny that resistance causes intense pain for their partner), they will usually open up and accept coaching.

Phlegmatics are usually resistant to the second step of the Process because of all the energy that must be expended to complete the step. They take the path of least resistance. They would rather smooth things over and just keep bumping along than challenge a familiar routine. Given a major crisis in the relationship—a crisis that threatens the relationship itself—they are likely to shrug their shoulders and say, "Well, I've done everything I know how to do." When they realize they've failed, they simply run the white flag up the flagpole. The possibility of changing patterns or investing major amounts of time and energy in new approaches (like self-assessment and journaling) is simply foreign to them.

Sanguines can be independent, dependent, or a mixture of the two. It depends on the moment. They are hard to pin down. They are all about forward momentum, and disinclined to examine the past. They are like Dory in the film *Finding Nemo:* Their motto is "Just keep swimming." They have a deep need for people and relationships. They are highly likely to offer a superficial "I forgive you" response to a crisis in the relationship without having experienced all the emotions necessary to merit that choice to forgive. Their too-hasty pronouncements of "forgiveness" papers over problems—and often leads to even deeper crises in the relationship.

STUDY QUESTIONS

Do you have any beliefs about yourself or the world that have supported the perpetuation of a false identity or persona? If so, what are those?

Are there any internal obstacles—such as a desire to please others at any cost, or a need to compete and win—that are preventing you from "digging up" old experiences, assumptions, and behavior patterns that result in choices that don't support you or your partner?

Are there any examples of you avoiding known issues in your relationship in order to "move on," "turn the page," or "just get on with it"? If so, what are those issues? How do you think your partner would answer this question?

When we fail to address the root system of dysfunctional behavior patterns we often fall into a habit of dealing only with the surface issues. This is known as "mowing the lawn," because the act of mowing a lawn does nothing to remove the weeds or the root systems that support them. The weeds always grow back. What's an example of you mowing the lawn in your relationship but not pulling up the weeds?

What are some issues with one or both of your parents (or an adult guardian) that are currently playing out in your relationship with your partner?

Are there any important issues or experiences from your past that have been layered down, minimized, or buried? If so, what are they? How do you think your partner would answer this question?

When difficult issues arise, do you ever deflect them? If so, how?

What are your propensities when it comes to handling stressful situations or difficult moments in your relationship? How do you typically respond? What would your partner say your propensities are?

6

Forgiveness and Releasing of Judgment

IN SOME OF the examples I shared with you in the previous chapter, the step of journaling and self-assessment led easily, organically, and naturally into the step of forgiving parents and others (including ourselves) and then releasing all judgments related to what happened to the person in childhood and adolescence.

Although that easy transition does happen on occasion, it is not the norm. The step of forgiving and releasing judgments typically takes a good deal more effort.

Very often, we take on a victim mindset in relation to something that happened to us in the past. This habit of looking at ourselves as the victim of someone or something else—be it a person or an event—is disempowering and unhealthy. It keeps us from growing and developing as human beings. In order to move past this mindset, we must complete the third step of the Process.

For instance, if a parent permitted us to take harmful drugs when we were too young to make good decisions on our own, and we did so, we must eventually reach the point where we authentically forgive that parent for his or her mistake, and in so doing release ourselves from the action of judging that parent, ever again, for having made that poor decision.

As a practical matter, this is impossible unless we have fully processed all the emotions arising from the experience of having taken drugs, having had a bad role model, having been made to feel unsafe, and so on. (This emotional processing, of course, is the work of the second step.) Yet even when we have experienced all the relevant emotions, important work remains to be done. **If we have experienced and dealt with the emotions, but we are still constantly replaying what went wrong and using what happened to perpetuate a story that envisions someone or something else as the cause of our problems in life, we will struggle in all our relationships.** Specifically, we will struggle in our most intimate relationship—the relationship with our spouse or partner.

It's important to note here that **forgiving someone does not mean approving of what they did, and releasing our judgments does not mean pretending there are no challenges in the relationship.** The third step of the Process is not about denial. What the third step accomplishes is *acknowledging and then consciously choosing to let go of what happened,* in exactly the same way we ask God to forgive us for the mistakes we have made in our lives.

"In prayer there is a connection between what God does and what you do. You can't get forgiveness from God, for instance, without also forgiving others. If you refuse to do your part, you cut yourself off from God's part" (Matthew 6:15, The Message).

This third step is all about freedom. Someone who has completed step two (journaling and self-assessment) but has not yet completed the third step (forgiveness and releasing of judgment) is still imprisoned by the past experience. **Anyone or anything that controls our emotions imprisons us.** Consistently living and reliving the reality of anger or bitterness or hatred or any other negative emotion toward someone who made a choice that affected our life is like drinking poison and expecting someone else to die as a result.

Forgiveness and releasing of judgment frees us from the toxic cycle of sin and brokenness. It means we step away from the confinement of reliving what happened to us in our past. With God's help, we build a new life—a life of freedom from judgment.

God says if we forgive, we will be forgiven. If we stay in the place of anger and bitterness, if we make justifications for remaining there, we are making the mistake of justifying ourselves. God wants to give us His justification, which is total freedom. Which justification do we really want to hold on to? Ours? Or God's?

"TELL ME WHAT YOU'RE FEELING"

For much of our marriage, Tyler wasn't very good at sharing his emotions. I would be trying to talk to Tyler, and I would run into this instant opposition. I would say things like, "What's on your mind? What's going on? What's bothering you?" Because I could tell by his body language that there was something wrong, and I would reach out to him and ask him to express his feelings, often because I wanted to find out whether it was something I had done that had caused the problem. But he wouldn't open up. He would just say that everything was fine and he would change the subject.

That pattern extended all the way into the period where we were involved in the Process together, but it took a very difficult turn for me then. I knew one of the reasons Tyler had a problem with telling me what he was feeling was that in his family, sharing feelings really wasn't something that was encouraged. In particular, his mother had been very closed down emotionally, and had hardly ever shared how she felt about anything that was happening.

So now, after we had spent some time working with Pastor Bill, we knew each other's temperaments fairly well, and we had a deeper sense of each other's personal history, and when we were at home together I would encourage him to open up and share what he was going through. I probably did that more often now, because I knew how important it was to share the feelings we were experiencing.

But I could tell there were times that he was upset about something and he just wasn't willing or able to tell me how he was feeling. He would still keep things to himself, and now there was a certain emotional edge to his responses.

I would say something to him like, "Come on, don't be like your mother; tell me what you're feeling." And he would just explode at me, which hadn't happened before. I found out later that a big part of the reason for these outbursts was what he was working through during the forgiveness step with Pastor Bill. Tyler would have been in the process of writing about something in longhand, which is one of the assignments Pastor Bill gives when it comes to forgiveness, and he just hadn't completed processing everything he was writing about. And then I would ask him to open up, and he just had these very intense emotional reactions. I never felt like I was in danger, or like he was in any way aggressive toward me as a person. But I could tell he was going through something major.

Once I confirmed with Bill that the main reason for these intense emotional reactions was him processing what had happened to him earlier in his life, I learned how to give him the space he needed while he was going through the act of forgiving people. It was not necessarily an easy transition for either of us, but we both did come out the other side. Going through that with Tyler taught me that forgiveness is not a passive thing; it's something people have to process emotionally, and it takes some effort and it's likely to engage some very intense emotions. But the thing is, once he went through that, he actually was able to tell me how he was feeling about things—which was an incredible gift. —Melanie

CAN YOU HANDLE REPENTANCE AND THE RELEASING OF JUDGMENT?

The whole idea of *repentance,* as in repenting of judgment toward parents and others, can be scary for some people. It is often perceived as primarily a religious word, but if you trace down the etymology, it simply means *regret.* In the sense in which we're using it, "repent" means nothing more or less than regretting a course of action deeply enough to change course, to turn around from the direction in which you're going. In this case, we're talking about noticing that you are judging someone else, and then choosing not to do that. To use contemporary parlance, **repenting of your judgment against others can be considered as being roughly synonymous with "doing a 180."** It means noticing that you're going in the wrong direction and then doing a U-turn.

Even with that explanation, though, I find many of the people I work with, especially those who have grown up with strong religious backgrounds, respond negatively to the word *repent.* Whenever this happens, I urge people to think about the idea of repenting of judgement as being identical to *releasing* the judgment against the other person. You had it once. Now you let it go. Releasing judgement effectively, in my experience, involves acknowledging the existence of some higher power and appealing to that power to do the judging that you are letting go . . . but this releasing of judgment does not require you to hold any fixed religious beliefs or follow any religious tradition. All it requires you to do is abandon the belief that you can or should be the judge and jury of someone else's life.

Whatever word we use, the key principle to take on is that **we must turn away from the path of indulging our own judgement on other people—even people who may have hurt us—leaving the final judgement on such matters to the higher power.** It is not our job to issue verdicts or sentences. It is our job to learn lessons, set appropriate boundaries, and move on in our lives.

Releasing judgment is an explicit, conscious choice to hand the job of judging over to the higher power. Like forgiveness, however, it is not a one-and-done proposition. It is something you will need to refine, repeat, and renew over time.

The reason this step is so very important is that we as human beings have a blind spot. When we believe someone has hurt us, when we believe someone has made a mistake, when we believe someone has acted improperly or selfishly or heedlessly, we are often naturally drawn to the act of judging them—of making sure they "get what they deserve." Experiencing this instinct to judge someone else is part of the human condition. The problem here is if we indulge that instinct, we often make things a great deal worse for ourselves and those around us. To fulfill our highest purpose as human beings we must constantly practice not just letting go, but also letting God handle the tricky business of judgment. We are simply too imperfect to get it right.

For most of us, authentic forgiveness and complete releasing of judgment does not come quickly or easily. But it is definitely worth the effort.

There's something about the act of taking personal responsibility and releasing people from judgement that means we are no longer bound to those judgements. Jesus told us not to judge because the judging can come back on us: **"For you'll be judged by the same standard that you've used to judge others. The measurement you use on them will be used on you"** (Matthew 7:2, the Passion Translation).

There is always suffering under the weight of judgement. The suffering always takes place in our own hearts. We may cloak it with various disguises (self-righteousness is a popular one) but the suffering always remains—until we forgive and release judgment.

This is not some mysterious or ethereal principle we're talking about here. It's a simple fact. When we take on the personal responsibility to release someone from a position where we have been blaming them, we simply remove something that was dysfunctional. It's like taking out the garbage.

This is not about anyone "getting away" with anything. The people we had previously been blaming are just doing what they're doing. They are broken, too, just like us.

They don't know any better. To imagine that they were doing it specifically against us, as part of some elaborate plot focused on us that they now want to "get away with," is not a useful or functional way to go through life. We are not prosecutors. This is not the criminal justice system. Let the people whose job it is to figure out whether someone needs to be prosecuted for a crime do their job. In the meantime, we need to do ours, which is forgiving and releasing from judgment We are responsible for our actions. The people we have been blaming are responsible for theirs. **If we choose not to forgive, we remain a victim, controlled by our own narrative. This is a dysfunctional choice.**

To be sure, it is also a very popular choice—a choice we can find evidence of many others buying into, and a choice we can easily justify making in our own lives if we so choose. But at some point we need to ask ourselves: How is that choice working out for us? In effect, we become "volunteer victims."

As Shannon put it, "*I had to learn to give it to God and stop trying to fix the lives of others, stop letting their actions determine my emotions.*"

Shannon's experience in the forgiveness step is particularly instructive when it comes to illuminating the step of **taking one's own thoughts captive,** a concept that can seem intimidating at first. In support of that step—which we will discuss in depth in the next chapter, but which I am covering here as well because it is often intertwined with the third step—I used an approach known as Rational Emotive Behavioral Therapy, or REBT for short. This is a pragmatic, results-focused form of therapy that encourages people to identify thoughts and feelings that don't support them, explore whether those thoughts and feelings really make sense, and then replace them with more productive, rational ways of looking at themselves at the world. REBT can be highly effective here in the third step. As Shannon put it:

> I had always thought of my thinking as being something that was out of my control, as something that just happened. When Bill started sharing the REBT therapeutic approach with me, I finally had a scaffolding in place that allowed me to take control of how I think. My melancholy temperament needed a way to analyze my thoughts, so that I could understand what was not supporting me in my old thought patterns and get a better sense of how to think and act on situations in a healthier way moving forward. In the past, I was the captive of my own thoughts—not the other way around. My mind was filled with dogmatic beliefs that arose from things my family did. I would think, "How dare they hurt me. They shouldn't be drinking. They shouldn't be doing this and they shouldn't be doing that."
>
> Bill helped me to understand that all my anxiety stemmed from what I was thinking and feeling about what people did and what they didn't do. If my dad drank, I would be anxious. If my mom didn't wish me a happy birthday, I would be anxious. By using REBT and cognitive therapy, I found I could control my thought process and therefore control how I responded to things. Previously, this would have been hard or impossible for me, because my emotions would get wildly out of control and I could not control my crying, breathing, or even keep food down. It took a lot of practice. REBT and discussions with Bill was

what gave me that practice.

That journal entry from Shannon is a portrait of forgiveness itself. It is what forgiveness and repenting of judgment looks like in action. In her case, forgiveness could not take place until she had begun the difficult task of taking her own thoughts captive. Shannon's story illustrates the sobering reality that a *failure* to take your thoughts captive can lead to depression, anxiety, codependency[2], and other mental health issues. That was exactly what Shannon experienced.

There came a point where I said to Shannon, "Do you realize that *all* of your trouble stems from your thoughts and your reactions to what other people do and say—and what they *don't* do and say?" There was a long pause, and her eyes grew wide. She got it. It was at that moment that she became committed to taking her own thoughts captive, because up to that point, her thoughts had been taking *her* captive. If your thoughts are taking you captive, as opposed to the other way around, the consequences in your life may lead to some very serious problems.

We will be looking more closely at the vitally important act of taking thoughts captive in the next chapter.

FORGIVENESS VS. RECONCILIATION

Many people look at a situation like Shannon's—a situation where there are still a lot of unresolved issues with parents and others—and ask this question: "Is that really forgiveness?

There's nothing wrong with therapy, of course, and nothing wrong with learning how to ask questions about your own thought process and change it for the better . . . but doesn't forgiveness require you to

---

2   By "codependency," I mean not only the traditional understanding of enabling a dysfunctional behavior pattern between people, but also the more common contemporary definition, which includes leaning on someone else's emotions and behaviors to determine your own sense of self-worth and identity. If your sense of self-worth depends on the actions, emotions, or behavior of another person, that is codependency.

have some kind of improvement in the relationship you have with the person you're forgiving, some sort of reconciliation?"

It surprises them to learn that the answer to that question is "No."

It is indeed possible to forgive someone and withhold reconciliation. It's also possible to forgive someone and have reconciliation withheld by that individual. It's even possible to forgive someone when we know that there is literally no opportunity for reconciliation—as is the case when we forgive someone who has passed away. Forgiveness and reconciliation are two different things. Forgiveness is always required by God, but forgiveness does not always lead to reconciliation.

It's possible, for instance, for forgiveness to occur in the context of Shannon's relationship with someone who she feels hurt her entirely separate from any contact with that person. This is healthy in that it indicates the need to establish boundaries—another aspect of her life that Shannon was also working to establish. Forgiveness is about releasing our own instinct to judge. Reconciliation is focused on restoring broken relationships and rebuilding trust. In situations where trust has been deeply broken, restoration is a process—sometimes, a lengthy one.

Unlike forgiveness, reconciliation is often conditioned on the attitude and actions of the offender. While its aim is restoration of a broken relationship, that aim is not always attainable, and when it is, it can take a while—especially in the case of relationships where there have been significant and repeated breaches of trust. If someone who has done wrong is genuinely repentant, they will recognize and accept that the mere act of apologizing is no guarantee of reconciliation. The wounds will take some time to heal. The offender's attitudes and actions may accelerate, or slow down, that healing process.

In many cases, even if an offender has confessed his wrong to the one he hurt in a heartfelt way and appealed for forgiveness, the offended person will still be obliged, in honesty, to say something like the following: "I forgive you, but it might take some time for me to regain trust and restore our relationship." Notice the distinction between whether the individual is forgiven (meaning the person who has been wronged is releasing the urge to judge) and whether the relationship is back to normal (it's not). The evidence of genuine forgiveness is personal freedom from a vindictive or vengeful response. That does not, however, mean that there has been an automatic restoration of the relationship.

Yes, being forgiven, restored, and trusted is an amazing experience, but it's important for us to understand that when we hurt others—and particularly when we hurt our spouse—it is not the other person's obligation to declare the relationship "fixed." Very likely, healing is a long way away, and what we do *after* we are forgiven will determine whether the trust is rebuilt and the relationship is restored. Words alone are usually not enough to restore trust and heal wounds. **When someone has been significantly hurt and feels hesitant about restoration with their offender, it's both right and wise to look for changes in the offender before allowing the process of reconciliation to begin.** Notice that setting boundaries is a part of moving forward.

Forgiveness means I no longer judge you. I can forgive you even if I don't trust you. Reconciliation, by contrast, means I believe we have done the hard work necessary to heal the relationship. The process of forgiveness requires nothing more than an open heart. The process of reconciliation depends on the attitude of the offender and the offended, the depth of the betrayal, and the pattern of offense.

When an offended party works toward reconciliation, the first and most important step is the confirmation of genuine repentance on the part of the offender. This is because reconciliation requires trust—trust that the person is genuine in their remorse, trust that they take responsibility, and trust that God's grace is sufficient when mine isn't enough.

Reconciliation is an extraordinary achievement, an achievement requiring effort and good will from two or more people. It would be nice if reconciliation could happen in every situation where someone was wronged, but the reality of human life is that it can't happen all the time, any more than a bridge can always be counted on to materialize whenever we want to cross a body of water. We have to build the bridge. Sometimes the body of water is too wide for a bridge to be built.

Forgiveness, on the other hand, is both a personal obligation and an act of selflessness. It is an act of will, a conscious act of obedience to God, not a whim of passing emotion. When we forgive we let go of the right to hang on to bitterness. We no longer hold on to our perceived right to be angry.

Forgiveness is what God requires of us. When we don't forgive, we suffer. If we are choosing to hold on to resentment, bitterness, anger, self-justifications, and rage, that decision will work against us. Forgiveness *can* happen in any and every situation where we feel we have been wronged . . . but it is always up to us whether or not it *does* happen. We must reconcile internally and get things right with ourselves first. Once we do, it becomes possible for us to get things right with other people.

"If you forgive others their trespasses, your heavenly Father will also forgive you, but if you do not forgive others their trespasses, neither will your Father forgive your trespasses" (Matthew 6:14–15).

STUDY QUESTIONS

We all play the victim from time to time. How does the victim mind-set manifest in your life?

When we are unforgiving of others, there is usually a judgment attached to that. Who is someone in your life who is unforgiven, someone toward whom you still hold a judgmental attitude? What does that judgment sound like and feel like?

If you had to identify one important person in your life whom you have not forgiven, who would that person be? How has that lack of forgiveness affected you and/or your relationship? What is standing in the way of forgiving that person?

Who do you still hold in judgment in your life? (Make a list.) Are you one of those people? What would it take for you to release those people from judgment?

Have you ever instinctively justified yourself or your actions in the relationship in a way that you eventually regretted doing? What form did that justification take?

What fears do you have that prevent you from communicating openly about your feelings with your partner?

Are there any areas in your relationship where you feel your partner has a blind spot—a habitual response pattern of dysfunction that he or she simply does not recognize or acknowledge? List as many of these as you can.

Is it possible you also might have such a blind spot? If so, what might one of those blind spots be? How would your partner answer this question?

What are some ways that you allowed the emotions and behaviors of others to control you when you were younger? What are some examples of this taking place in your adult life?

Can you think of a time when your instinctive thought patterns and emotional reactions really did not serve you because they did not give you a rational assessment of the situation you faced?

What is the difference between forgiveness and reconciliation?

Have you ever had difficulty forgiving someone because you thought you had to reconcile with them first? Describe what that situation was like, and what it would take for you to forgive the person now.

Has there been a situation where a lack of forgiveness has caused suffering in your life or the lives of others?

7
Taking Thoughts Captive

A **SPECIAL WORD** of explanation is in order about the fourth step of the Process, taking thoughts captive. This step is likely to unfold in tandem with or shortly after the completion of the third step, forgiveness, but as a practical matter it can take place at any point in the Process.

This essential, deeply personal step is inspired and illuminated by a memorable passage in one of Paul's epistles: **"We demolish arguments and every pretension that sets itself up against the knowledge of God, and we take captive every thought to make it obedient to Christ" (2 Corinthians 10:5 NIV).**

In other words, **sustainable change and growth depend on the changes you apply to your everyday life, relationships, *and thought patterns*.** These changes stem from a deep inward transformation. They are not sustainable unless they are accompanied by mental transformations that occur inwardly and are expressed outwardly. This is the essence of taking thoughts captive.

Boiled down into a single sentence, this fourth step sounds pretty simple in theory: **Accept that you don't have to believe or obey everything you think.**

In other words, we need to learn to examine our own thoughts, step away from them for a moment, and determine for ourselves whether our habitual, recurrent patterns of thought support us and our partners . . . or don't. If they don't support us, we can change them, challenge them, and redesign them so that they do support us. Our thoughts are great servants, but lousy masters. Accepting this is a personal breakthrough without which the rest of the Process will prove difficult and, ultimately, impossible.

As I have mentioned, this step is often intertwined with the third step, forgiveness and releasing of judgment. Each individual is different, however, and one's temperament has a lot to do with the optimal timing and mentor support required to master the step of taking thoughts captive. What is essential, however—regardless of one's temperament, one's relationship with the mentor, and one's personal history—is that we assume personal responsibility and control for our own thought life.

Most of us have fallen into the habit of instinctively believing everything we think. Mastering the fourth step of the process means not falling into this trap. We cannot be transformed if we have not yet learned how to take our own thoughts captive.

MARIE'S STORY

Years ago, when I first started doing this work, I mentored a young woman by the name of Marie. Marie was in recovery. I was mentoring her in her close personal relationships, and in her recovery as well. She was a melancholy compulsive (like me), meaning melancholy in all areas: inclusion, control, and affection. I remember how, during one session, I was talking to Marie about her thoughts, and coaching her to learn—just as I, a fellow melancholy compulsive, had learned—to step back and evaluate for herself whether her habitual thought processes were helping her in her relationships or in her recovery. After I had made this point for perhaps the twentieth time, and shared some of the examples from my own life of how I had been able to challenge my own thought processes and redesign them so they did a better job of serving me, something interesting happened. I saw a change in Marie's posture and facial expression. She went from being stressed and distracted to being curious and engaged. It was like a little light bulb had gone off inside her head.

Marie said, "I want to be sure I understand what you're telling me here. Are you saying I don't *have* to think this way?"

"Yes," I replied. "That's exactly what I'm saying."

That discussion marked the turnaround for Marie, in terms of both her family and romantic relationships and her path toward recovery. Prior to that moment, she had fallen into the common trap of believing that her thoughts were *reality*—that she couldn't change them, that they were simply there, and that they reflected what was actually taking place in her world. This is a particularly important myth to bust for people (like me) with melancholy temperaments. We think all the time. We are dominated by our own thought life.

It doesn't naturally occur to us that our own thoughts are something we can challenge, revise, and assume personal, conscious control over. But we can. It's difficult in the beginning, but with practice, we can learn to assert full control over our own thought life. Anyone can.

We are talking about a central, but elusive, element of self-awareness: noticing our own thoughts *as thoughts,* as opposed to assuming they are what is actually taking place in our lives. If we can notice thought patterns, identify where they are coming from, become more certain about when they are most likely to show up for us and what effect they are likely to have on us, *we can do something about them.* For instance, if Marie has a common thought response to aggression from others that says, "I deserve this," she doesn't have to live with that as the reality of her life. She can notice when that internal response comes up, why it comes up, and what impact it has on her self-esteem and her relationships with others. And she can deepen her own self-awareness and set a new thought process in motion to replace the one that isn't supporting her. For instance: "I have a right to express myself, even in difficult situations." She now has given herself permission to do that.

As we think in our hearts, so we are. God has created us with inherent value. Any voice within us that attempts to convince us otherwise must be understood as a salvo in a spiritual battle with an enemy who constantly attempts to beat us down with a ceaseless wave of lies about our value, ability, potential, and so forth. We are warned not to be unwise to that enemy's schemes.

If we can notice our recurrent thought patterns and understand their impact on us, then we can also do something about them. Our minds are like a landing field. We're used to having the planes come in and land whenever they want. They land and unload their cargo and they put all kinds of crates and boxes and shipping containers wherever they feel like putting them. We sit in the control tower, doing nothing. We issue no instructions, offer no guidance, use no system and no criteria for identifying what we want, or don't want, from those planes—or where we want, or don't want, cargo to be stored. Our thoughts are what's inside those boxes the planes have gotten into the habit of dumping all over the airfield. One day, it occurs to us: We don't have to take every flight, and we don't have to let every plane unload its cargo. We can tell the pilots whether and where we want them to land. We can tell them whether we want the cargo they feel like unloading. We can get out there with our checklist and our clipboard before the plane is even unloaded, and we can look the pilot in the eye and say, "Excuse me—we need to identify what's in these boxes before we give you permission to unload."

TAKING THOUGHTS CAPTIVE IS NOT EASY

Most of us are not used to the act of taking our own thoughts captive. It doesn't come naturally to us. We need a little practice. The mentor's role in making sure we get this practice, through activities during and between face-to-face sessions, is absolutely essential. **The mentor helps us to build up the "muscle" that makes taking thoughts captive second nature.** Building up that muscle is easier once we have forgiven ourselves and others—which is why I have placed this step where I have in the book, following the forgiveness step.

Practicing the initially difficult work of taking our thoughts captive—learning to proactively evaluate what we choose to take on and believe from our own mental processes—can be a major step toward personal healing, especially when the practice arises from a place of forgiveness. Without forgiveness, the practice we put in, even under the guidance of a mentor, is likely to result in frustration and stress. With forgiveness, that practice can point us toward a constructive response to the developmental trauma we experienced while growing up.

Taking our thoughts captive, from a place of forgiveness, may well be the *only* constructive response we can make on a personal level if we have experienced developmental trauma. That trauma may take the form of abandonment, parental inversion (having to take on the role of the adult while we are still a child), neglect, abuse, sexual trauma, or any of dozens of other examples of trauma that may be affecting us as we attempt to navigate life as adults.

If we do not learn to take control of our own thoughts as they relate to the trauma we experienced as children we are highly unlikely to heal that trauma as adults. Instead, we will rely on "coping and hoping," the superficial "work-arounds" we have created over the years and use now to cover up the insecurities and dysfunction caused by the trauma we have experienced. We may even end up entering a cycle of addiction to numb the pain arising from our developmental trauma. Addictions then layer on top of, and compound, our existing issues. The bottom line is that our reliance on coping mechanisms makes healing impossible and causes a multitude of areas of brokenness that will be present as we move on in life. Only taking control of our own thoughts, from a place of forgiveness, will allow us to identify and take the steps necessary to actually heal the trauma we have experienced.

People often ask me why they should make the effort to forgive, why they should make the effort to turn around the ingrained habits of a lifetime and do the hard work of practicing taking control of their own thoughts. The best answer I have to offer is that if we leave our trauma unhealed we will increase the odds that our brokenness will be passed down from generation to generation. This cycle can, and too often does, go on for generations. No one wants that. Once we are confronted with our dysfunction, and find we cannot sustain relationships that work, we will do well to seek out a mentor who can help us discover the areas of trauma and help lead us through a journey of healing that includes practice in forgiveness and practice in taking our own thoughts captive. In this way, we can find the freedom to become the person we were truly meant to be—and we can finally break the generational chain of brokenness and dysfunction. Our efforts will have been well worth it.

There is a good deal to learn about taking one's own thoughts captive in this powerful parable from the Gospel of Luke:

> *When the unclean spirit has gone out of a man, he roams through waterless places in search of rest; and finding none, he says, "I will return to my house which I left." And when he has come to it, he finds the place swept and clean. Then he goes and takes seven other spirits more evil than himself, and they enter in and dwell there; and the last state of that man becomes worse than the first. (Luke 11:24–25)*

Let's take a moment to unpack what is happening in this parable. For "unclean spirit," read "dysfunctionality and brokenness." We all have some dysfunctionality; we all have some kind of brokenness. With effort, self-awareness, and support, we can recognize these negative cycles for what they are and make choices that expel them from our lives. The real trick, however, is *keeping* these patterns of thought and behavior expelled. Getting our minds "swept and clean" is only the beginning. When we learn to consciously evaluate what we choose to believe, and make our minds our servant, rather than our master, we can fill up the spaces with forgiveness, compassion, and love. We must learn to cultivate thoughts that fill the spaces, so the areas of bitterness and disconnection that were present before do not have the opportunity to return in an even worse form. We really can fill those spaces with love—once we grasp and act on the reality that we do not have to believe everything we think. Choosing which thoughts we will "unpack" may take effort, and it may not feel natural at first, but it is what allows us to make sure we don't replace one wave of dysfunctionality and brokenness with seven more layers that leave us in an even worse place.

Why is this so important? Because without taking our thoughts captive we are dead in the water. We are leaning on our own understanding.

That's what we have gotten used to doing, and so it's what we do pretty much all of the time: We use our own base of experience to determine what something happening in our lives *means.* We react emotionally, and we believe what we think about that emotional experience. We impose our subjective understanding of what we are going through. What if there's a bigger picture we're just not seeing? What if we could step back and try to get a sense of the places where what we believe about a given situation may be falling short?

"Trust in the LORD with all your heart and lean not on your own understanding" (Proverbs 3:5).

Those words you just read lie at the heart of the essential skill of not believing everything you think, not accepting at face value everything your thought life presents to you. Practicing this skill is part of being a functional human being. If it is missing, then an important part of our maturity as adults is also missing. I had to learn, years ago, to get into the habit of asking myself a couple of essential questions: "What if I am wrong here? What if I am missing something?" I had to learn to evaluate my own thoughts and determine whether those thoughts included some kind of judgment against someone else—or against myself, with me then taking the disappointment in myself out on someone else.

Very often, I found there was some kind of judgment taking place, and I had to practice giving the other person, or myself, the benefit of the doubt. All of this is a matter of humbling oneself and putting one's ego aside, which doesn't come about automatically. It takes time. I know, because it has taken me a long time to begin to get past my own broken, insecure need to be right all the time!

I work with many, many people whose automatic first response to any perceived problem in their marriage, or anywhere else in their life, is to try to solve everything on their own, to try to define reality on their own terms, based on their own experience and their own emotions, and basically beat themselves half to death with the stick of their own understanding. Over the years, I and other mentors have come to call this self-focused approach "three-fiving it"—meaning that the person we're talking to has forgotten, for the moment, about the important lesson waiting for everyone in Proverbs, verse three, chapter five. The advice we offer here is actually pretty simple: "Stop three-fiving it!" Stop pretending your own understanding is the final word on what is happening in your marriage, in your life, or in the world at large.

Here is an example of what I mean. Years ago, when I went back to school for counseling, I was in my forties. I hadn't been in any kind of ongoing educational environment as a student since high school. I came back from the first day of classes with a big stack of books. My wife asked me, "How did it go?"

I said, "Fine, but I don't think I'm going to be able to pull it off. I've always been a lousy student."

She looked at me for a long moment, then she said, "You used to be a lousy student. You're not a lousy student anymore. Why can't you be an excellent student?"

She was absolutely right. I was three-fiving it. I had a limiting thought pattern, deeply woven into my mind, my assumptions, and my image of myself, called "lousy student." I wasn't brought up in an environment where I had learned to even think of myself as an excellent student. I was brought up to think, "That's a pretty cool idea, but I can't do that." That kind of limiting thought pattern, I came to understand, was something I had a moral obligation to *disobey*. I had to learn to notice that thought pattern, step away from it, and open myself up to a new set of perceptions and a new outlook—an outlook that transformed my expectations of myself. Now my outlook is: The Bible tells me that I can do all things through Christ, who strengthens me. What would someone who was strengthened by Christ do in the situation I face?

Noticing the old, dysfunctional, unsupportive thought cycles, and replacing them with better thought patterns, better questions, and better assumptions, is the essence of taking your own thoughts captive. And it can change your life.

Your expectations are not reality. Neither are your resentments or your justifications or your internal narratives about what events mean. How could they be? Whatever your understanding of God may be, or even if you have no belief in God, good old common sense should tell you that your own perceptions cannot possibly be the final word on all things.

Too often, the way we habitually think about ourselves and the world around us keeps us in a box of hopelessness, anger, and judgment against ourselves and others. We can change that at any time.

CHANGING OUR THOUGHT LIFE

We really do not have to remain locked into our own habitual patterns of thought. We can learn to identify them, step back from them, figure out where they have come from, and decide for ourselves whether or not they serve us. We can create, and live, a consciously designed thought life. One particularly powerful story of someone who did this successfully was Sean.

Sean grew up in a household where his father withheld his approval and acted as though his son had never measured up and never would measure up. That was a rough beginning, but things got even worse in school, where Sean was bullied relentlessly.

From a very early age, then, Sean found himself under assault. He did what most of us would do when we find ourselves assaulted, both physically and emotionally, on a regular basis: He looked for ways to survive.

It was a matter of survival that caused him to search out a new identity for himself, an identity that could protect him from emotional assaults at home and physical assaults at school. As it happened, Sean had some gifts as an athlete, and when the opportunity presented itself to distinguish himself as a baseball player, he threw himself into the game. He told me, "I thought that ballplayers were respected, so I decided to become a ballplayer."

Sean imagined that success on the ball field would translate into a cease-fire from the bullies who had been tormenting him. Unfortunately, he was wrong about that. The bullying continued, even after he had created a good record of success as a baseball player and a new identity for himself as an athlete.

So Sean made another transition. He created yet another identity: the tough guy, the fighter. If people were going to pick on him, he would transform himself into the person who attacked first. He threw himself into that identity as well. Again, it was a matter of survival. But the new identity came at a heavy cost: Sean's own sense of self. "There was a baseball player over here, and a fighter over there, but in between, there was just a void," he told me. "I had absolutely no idea who I was."

Sean went through a rough period, and eventually landed in the military, which turned out to be both a variation on the "fighter" persona and an exercise in total conformity and total submission that made the void at the center of his life grow even wider. "In order for me to survive in the military, I had to be like everyone else, and I had to do what they told me to do. But there was still this emptiness in the center of my life, even when I got out of the military."

Sean had to come to terms with lingering bitterness about being bullied as a child, and about problems connected to his relationship with his parents. Only when he was able to reach a point of forgiveness with people from his past was he able to approach his own thinking patterns critically and objectively and see how they were limiting him in his communication with his wife Kayla. As a choleric, Sean already had a predisposition toward intense and angry responses when she tried to share constructive criticism; in these situations, he came to realize, he saw his wife as a potential adversary, as a threat to be neutralized. Needless to say, this response was a challenge to their ability to connect!

Like a lot of people who go through challenging childhoods, Sean was a textbook example of arrested emotional development. In his early thirties, he still carried with him all of the attitudes and instincts that he had used to get through the experiences of parental disapproval, being bullied, and his military experience.

Those attitudes and instincts can be summarized into one grim sentence: "I have to find a way to survive this."

Because of his (understandable!) fixation on survival, Sean's maturation had literally stopped. He had yet to learn adult patterns of behavior (like compromise and curiosity) that most people pick up in adolescence and young adulthood to navigate personal relationships. Thanks to the work he has done on taking his own thoughts captive, he is now much more comfortable with transforming the potential weaknesses of his temperament—aggression and combativeness, heightened in his case by an adrenaline-fueled belief that life itself is at stake—into the classic choleric strength of appropriate assertiveness. Not only that, but whereas before he was routinely seeing others—including his wife—as an adversary to be defeated, he is now sharing feelings and making compromises, activities that he once saw as synonymous to showing weakness to an adversary.

Let me emphasize: This progress only came about after Sean had reached a point of forgiveness toward his parents and others who had hurt him when he was younger. Before that forgiveness came about, there was no forward motion on transforming his own thought life. It didn't matter how closely he examined the root system. Without the experience of forgiveness, he was unable to let go of the old issues, and unable to challenge and revise his own thought processes. (For instance, he was unable to let go of the preconception that expressing how he felt to his wife was a sign of vulnerability toward an adversary who was likely to harm him.)

Having made that transition to forgiveness, he was able to begin an important new phase of his life's journey. He has cleaned out the house. Now his job is to keep the "demons"—the broken and dysfunctional patterns of behavior—from returning. He must keep the house clean and well swept. Taking his thoughts captive is the primary means by which he is doing that.

Sean told me: "Because I chose to take on personal responsibility for my own thoughts, I am no longer identified by my past—I know who I am, and I'm free to 'be.' Actually, I am in the process of discovering who I am." By changing his thought life, he has changed his life!

What Sean accomplished, with the support of an experienced mentor—what you and your partner can accomplish, with the support of an experienced mentor—is perfectly encapsulated in the following powerful words:

> "So here's what I want you to do, God helping you: Take your everyday, ordinary life—your sleeping, eating, going-to-work, and walking-around life—and place it before God as an offering. Embracing what God does for you is the best thing you can do for him. Don't become so well-adjusted to your culture that you fit into it without even thinking. Instead, fix your attention on God. You'll be changed from the inside out. Readily recognize what he wants from you, and quickly respond to it. Unlike the culture around you, always dragging you down to its level of immaturity, God brings the best out of you, develops well-formed maturity in you." (Romans 12:1–2, The Message translation)

Sean's world placed certain pressures and certain assumptions on him, just as it places pressures and assumptions on everyone. It was squeezing him into a corner. We all run the risk of becoming so well adjusted to that world that is out to squeeze us into a corner that we begin to fit in without even thinking. But by learning to question our own thought life, we can reach a point where becoming the best version of ourselves is not just possible, but what we actually experience, day by day.

WE ARE ALL WORKS IN PROCESS

Committing fully to the step of taking our own thoughts captive means accepting, as Sean has accepted, that the task of discovering who we really are, how we have been limiting ourselves, and how we can best learn and grow in our lives is an ongoing business, something that is never complete. **We will never "finish" the job of evaluating whether or not we should believe what we are thinking about ourselves and others. We are all works in process.**

We are not talking about some magical, instant transformation. We are talking about steady, predictable progress toward a pattern of stepping back to make informed, mature, considered responses to our own thought patterns . . . to our environment . . . and to the people who matter in our lives, starting with our spouse. This kind of progress is very likely to be of the two-steps-forward, one-step-back variety. And that is fine. If you take a moment to consider all the areas where you learned to master a new and important skill—riding a bike, doing a new job, parenting—you will realize that two steps forward, one step back is the way that you, and the rest of the human beings on earth, learn best. We make mistakes. We learn from those mistakes. We change what wasn't working, and we replace it with something that works better.

Let me conclude this chapter by observing that it would be a mistake to think that anyone—up to and including the mentor you will be working with—has it all together. Because we are human beings, we are never "complete." We are never "done" doing the work of capturing our own thoughts. The mentor may have been around for a while, may have been through multiple life situations, may have grown on any number of levels, and may be able to help others learn how to avoid or get out of bad situations. That mentor is still alive, still human, and still going through the process of life, just like everyone else.

Probably 98 percent of the help I might offer people is born out of having received help myself in situations that have taught me about them. That direct experience is much more relevant than any counseling technique, or any degrees on my wall. Not only that, since I am still alive, I am prone to many of the same thought-life mistakes and pitfalls as the people I counsel. Yes, I avoid many of these mistakes because I have learned, grown, matured, and acquired some wisdom over the years, but I am not impervious to difficulty in relationships, to decision-making errors, to responding poorly to others, and so on.

The great mystic and writer, Henri Nouwen, provides us with several quotes that exemplify this reality. I have reproduced them below:

> "We don't sit as those who have all the answers, but journey together toward light and liberation."

> "Do we want to get useful information, or do we want to show that someone else is wrong? Do we want to conquer knowledge, or do we want to grow in wisdom?"

> "I am learning to trust God's love and God's actions and spend less time worrying about things I don't need to 'know'. Sometimes it is OK—and good for the soul—to be left in the dark. I am more prone to humble myself and accept leadership to help me out of the dark place."

> "Why can't we just be content with not knowing all the answers? After all, if we knew everything God knows, we wouldn't need God; we would be God."

I would only add to Henri's wise words the observation that taking your thoughts captive is a lifelong step. Don't expect to complete it overnight. Don't expect to complete it at all. But do make a commitment to get better at it over time, with the help and support of your mentor. And remember that he or she is working on this, too.

STUDY QUESTIONS

Do you ever excuse or justify yourself by thinking or saying, "That's just the way that I am?" Describe a time that happened.

Taking one's own thoughts captive takes practice and persistence. Do you think it would be easier to learn to do it on your own, or with the help and support of a mentor? Explain your answer.

Contrary to popular belief, everyone has trauma (also known as "baggage") in their background. With that in mind, what is yours, and how has it kept you from being present in your own thought process? Describe the event(s) in as much depth as you can.

An addictive behavior is one that you may think you can stop anytime you want, but you can't, and that has an adverse effect on your life, your relationships, and your ability to fulfill important commitments. A popular misconception is that only drugs and alcohol are addictive, but there are many addictive behaviors that do not involve substance abuse: too much screen time, pornography, shopping, gambling, and so on. What is an example of an addictive behavior in your world that you use to cope? Explain your answer.

Can you identify any patterns in your life and relationships that reflect dysfunctional beliefs of behavior patterns that you recognize in the lives of either of your parents? Describe those patterns in as much depth as you can and discuss how they have affected your ability to forgive either or both of your parents. (If someone other than a parent raised you, write about each such person.)

What persistent assumptions, attitudes, and thought patterns are standing in the way of you forgiving important people from your past?

Think of someone from your past whom you have not been able to forgive. If you were speaking to a trusted third party or a mentor, what advice do you think that person would offer about this situation?

We often create alternative identities or personas as coping mechanisms. (Sean's story in this chapter is an example of that.) Can you think of a time in your life when you created a new version of yourself as a coping mechanism for dealing with past trauma or injury in your life? What identity did you create? Describe it in detail.

Do you ever treat your spouse as an adversary? Why or why not? What would your spouse say about this? Do you think your partner views you in the same light?

What social, family, or other pressures can lead you to revert to dysfunctional assumptions or patterns of behavior as "survival techniques"? Give specific examples.

How would you rate your ability to "bounce back" from problems and challenges in your relationships? Do setbacks discourage you, or do they inspire you to keep moving forward? Explain your answers, and give examples.

8
Effecting Inner Healing

THE FIFTH STEP of the Process, effecting inner healing, is placed relatively late in the sequence for a single, powerful reason: This is where the positive results in relationships and elsewhere tend to begin to be noticeable to the people taking part in the Process . . . and those results tend not to happen until they have done a good deal of work on themselves.

Like the fourth step, taking thoughts captive, there can be glimmers of evidence of effecting inner healing at any number of earlier points—but the *sustained* experience of this fifth step, the ability to put it into practice on a consistent basis, tends not to take place until the forgiveness and taking thoughts captive steps have been made part of the person's daily experience, thanks to regular sessions with a mentor.

None of which answers the question that is probably on your mind now, which is, I am guessing: What actually happens in the fifth step?

And the short answer to that is: **In the fifth step, you discover**

a clearer pathway to emotional freedom, and you start down that path, one step at a time.

In this part of the Process, you take all the work you have done thus far and you build on it, to the benefit of your own capacity to mature as a person. You begin taking all that work you've done with your mentor out of the theoretical realm and you bring it into the realm of self-awareness, the realm of noticing and conscious choosing. You internalize the lessons you have learned about yourself, your past, your temperament, and your spouse. You begin to notice the choices you are making, and you begin noticing whether those choices support you and your relationships. You start to recognize your authentic self, and you start getting a clearer understanding of exactly what it is that has kept you from expressing that authenticity up to this point. You start acting in accordance with the person you know, deep down, that you are really meant to be. You stop judging yourself and others so much.

You begin learning how to accept who you really are—a person with strengths, shortcomings, and a sense of purpose—and, wonder of wonders, you start learning how to embrace and transform your brokenness and turn it into strength. **You start learning to recognize and trust who you are on the inside and what your own best instincts are. You begin, in short, to make progress.**

When you begin learning how to live in that trusting way—and notice that I said *begin to learn,* because all of us are works in progress—you not only bring about (that is, "effect") inner healing of the wounds you may have accumulated beginning in your childhood years, but you also begin functioning more effectively in your relationships, starting with your relationship with yourself and then moving outward to your relationship with your significant other, and then to relationships with others. You begin to accept yourself. And, as a result, **when stressful situations arise, as they inevitably do, you start acting more like a grownup.**

The fifth step is not a magic wand. It's not a borderline you cross that automatically makes responding in a mature, compassionate, conscious way second nature to you. It is, however, a glimpse of what is possible in life when you learn to be present in your own thought processes and your own choices. And it is something you can get better at over time.

ONE ON ONE

I've mentioned already that, when we begin the Process for a couple seeking to improve their relationship, we begin with a single meeting in which both partners take part but we quickly move on to a phase of one-on-one sessions, encouraging each partner to do some serious self-assessment and reach a point of personal responsibility for their own life and choices before we go back to having both couples in the room together. There's a reason we do it that way, and avoid a traditional "marriage counseling" approach, in which each session is attended by both partners. The challenge I have with that approach is that typically all it yields is variations on the blame game: "She always does X, and if she just changed that, we wouldn't have any problems." "He never does Y, even though I've told him hundreds of times how important Y is to me. He simply can't listen to anyone else, because he's totally self-obsessed, and if he doesn't learn to pay attention to what someone else is actually saying and take action on it, I can't take any more of this." And so on.

We hear these kinds of pronouncements when a couple that is having problems sits down in front of the "marriage counselor" for a very simple reason: Neither partner has reached a point of accepting personal responsibility for owning their issues, either at home or in the workplace. As a result, if you ask either of them what the biggest problem in the relationship is, the answer is always to point at the other person. Experience has shown that helping people reach a point of assuming personal responsibility for their own issues is inevitably a private journey, undertaken with the benefit of coaching from an experienced mentor. So, the early sessions are each partner meeting individually with the mentor.

Those one-on-one sessions with the mentor typically continue until each partner begins to get a basic understanding of his or her temperament, of the unique root system present in his or her life, and of the areas where a lack of forgiveness may be keeping the person from objectively evaluating his or her own thought life and guiding assumptions. Once each partner begins to at least get a glimpse of what the current deficits are in each of these areas, joint sessions with the mentor have the potential to become more productive. And once each partner begins assuming personal responsibility for his or her own issues, *in the context of the relationship,* the blame game recedes and inner healing can begin.

When one partner is still addicted to a pattern of blaming behavior, or a pattern of playing the victim, effecting inner healing is impossible. However, once the person has begun to accept the unworkability of these patterns and has taken on full responsibility for his or her own issues and choices, past and present, this vitally important inner healing can begin. Like taking thoughts captive, effecting inner healing is often a two-steps-forward, one-step-back experience that unfolds over time—but that, of course, is how most meaningful personal change manifests in our lives. It is how we learn to discover who we really are, how we come to make important choices, and how we determine what is most important to us as individuals, as colleagues, and as partners.

Here is a true story from one of the people I've worked with closely that shows just how powerful the step of effecting inner healing can be.

The young man's name is Matt. Matt had been having sessions with me privately for months, and had followed a classic pattern: After significant self-examination, he came to terms with the trauma of his own past, reached a point where he knew he needed to forgive his parents, and began the difficult work of taking on his own responsibility for releasing judgments and forgiving, so as to move beyond victimhood, bitterness, and resentment.

Once he did that, he then began learning to take his own thoughts captive by assuming personal responsibility for assessing whether his own thought processes were supporting him. A classic Choleric, Matt began transforming the potential weaknesses of that temperament—impatience, anger, and a judgmental attitude—into mature Choleric strengths, such as directness, decisiveness, and a strong sense of right and wrong. Not only that, but in terms of affection, Matt's temperament was strongly Supine, the compassionate and tenderhearted aspect of which came more into play in his personal relationships. To oversimplify somewhat (but not by much), Matt began to get a sense of who he really was, and in which direction decisions supporting his true self—the person he was meant to be—really lay. Matt probably put it best when he said: "I stopped striving to reach my potential and started walking in my purpose."

And yet he realized that some of his life choices were not supporting that purpose, not supporting the person he knew he was really meant to be. Why? Because he had not had enough *practice* making choices that supported the person he was meant to be. Much of this was still theoretical for him. He had not yet effected inner healing—not yet made it a reality in his personal experience.

This point began to come up powerfully for Matt during our one-on-one sessions. He would tell me, for instance, that he felt like a "hypocrite." When I asked him why, he would say, "I feel like I am hiding all the work you and I are doing from my girlfriend Vanessa. I haven't mentioned a single word about the progress I am making here as a result of my discussions with you. I haven't said one thing about how important my spiritual life has become over the past few months, and there is a gnawing sense inside of me that not talking about that with Vanessa is a huge mistake. And that's just the tip of the iceberg. What is really bothering me is the feeling I have that our sexual relationship is just not in line with who I am, with who I think God wants me to be. I started out wanting sex from Vanessa; I made a mistake in getting physically intimate too soon, but now I don't know how to express that to her. And I feel like if I do express it to her, I risk losing her."

At this point I have to pause and point out that this kind of honest

self-assessment, and personal accountability, was a new way of thinking for Matt. When I started working with him, his predictable response
to problems in his personal life—indeed, to problems in any aspect
of his life—was a predictable two-step dance of a) get angry and b)
blame someone or something else for whatever was happening. That
wasn't his instinctive response to this situation. So already, he was on
a different path. The question before the house was how were Matt's
choices going to be different now?

How could he maintain that forward progress, effect inner healing,
and, as a direct result of that healing, make the choices that supported
him as a more mature, less dysfunctional person?

I told Matt that I could see that he had made a lot of progress,
and that it was now time to take what he had learned and put it into
practice. If there were important things that he had learned about
himself by pursuing the Process, then he had an obligation to share
those things directly and openly with Vanessa. Not only that, but if he
had been concealing important things from her—and working with
me definitely fell under that category—then he needed to bring those
things out into the open and admit the concealment. Last but certainly
not least, if he had strong feelings about whether it was appropriate or
wise for the two of them to be physically intimate at this stage of their
relationship, failing to have a discussion about that could only damage
their chances of building a successful life together.

Having shared all of that with Matt, I watched as he took a long
moment to process it all, to take it all in and decide what, if anything,
he was going to do in response to what I had just said. Ultimately, of
course, what mattered most was not what I had to say about Matt's
situation, but what he decided to do about it. As I watched him think
over what I had said, I couldn't help feeling that I was observing effecting inner healing in action.

As it happened, I was right. Matt told me that, even though he was
concerned about the possibility of losing Vanessa, he also realized that
continuing in the mistakes he had already made of concealing both
the work he was doing with me and the deep misgivings he was having

about their decision to be sexually intimate was an even greater risk. He resolved to tell Vanessa everything he had told me. He knew that to do otherwise would not be walking in his true purpose.

At first, Vanessa's response was strongly negative. How could he have kept something as important as talking to me secret? What exactly did he mean by suggesting they take sex off the table? And where on earth was all this talk about God coming from when he hadn't mentioned anything about spirituality making a difference to him in any of their previous conversations?

These were, to be sure, some intense discussions, and I would be lying if I said they had been easy for Matt. But **effecting inner healing is not always easy, and it often requires us to confront some risks— risks worth taking on behalf of our authentic self.** Matt took that risk by asking Vanessa to hear him out and accept him as he knew himself to be. And she not only opted to stay with him, but eventually chose to pursue the Process herself!

LOVE EVERY VERSION OF YOURSELF

The step of effecting inner healing does not come about instantly, and it typically does not come about without significant support, encouragement, and, yes, even an occasional in-your-face challenge from the mentor. It's quite common for someone I am working with to get complacent, resistant, or go into a phase of denial, even after a long period of working with me. We must turn the theoretical into the practical. If what we have learned about ourselves is not translated into actionable choices, if we persist in living in the way that has become familiar to us simply *because* it has become familiar to us, then we will find ourselves in a downward cycle—one that accelerates rapidly. On the other hand, if we are willing to put our actions where our words are, if we are willing to take the lessons we have learned about ourselves and our own thought processes and use them to create a new way of living, then we can make the healing in our lives a reality.

"If you persist in living your own way, you will eat the bitter fruit of living your own way" (Proverbs 1:31, The Living Bible).

Effecting inner healing is all about turning all our hard-earned insights into a new set of choices, a new way of living. The mentor can't do that for us. We always have to do it for ourselves, even though we may need the help of the mentor when it comes to recognizing how resistant to change we may be. To support the kind of transformation I'm talking about, it is quite common for the mentor to have to push a little bit—particularly in those cases where the client has come to rely on the mentor not just as a guide, but as an agent of change. The client must be the agent of change in his or her own life! No one can effect inner healing for you. You must take action on your own behalf.

I can remember many times when I have said something along the following lines to a client who was skeptical or resistant when the time came to effect inner healing: "You are the one who has to assign value to this—not me. The value is there. You've done enough work and brought yourself far enough along to know that. The question is not whether I can do something for you that you can't do for yourself. The question is whether you are going to make a deep commitment to act on fulfilling your own purpose."

An amazing thing happens when we make that commitment: We learn to love every version of ourselves. We learn to have compassion for ourselves. And once that process begins, we can begin learning to have compassion for other people.

This is not merely an essential prerequisite for healing an intimate relationship—it is the starting point for healing *any and every* relationship in our lives. We have to reach a point of acceptance with ourselves first.

PUT PURPOSE AT THE CENTER OF YOUR LIFE

Effecting inner healing allows you find out who you really are meant to be, and that allows you to place your purpose, your true reason for being, right at the center of your life. **Too often we try to place our career at the center of our life, or our personal interests or obsessions, or our values, or our abilities.** When we put any one of these things first in our lives we are setting ourselves up for a fall. Remember what Matt said about his own journey: "I stopped striving to reach my potential and started walking in my purpose." This transition, the transition toward identifying and walking in one's own purpose, is the essence of the fifth step. Discovering and acting on this purpose is what allows people to become leaders in their own lives.

When people don't know who they truly are or what they are truly meant to be and become, they tend to fixate on externals. This eventually leads to some kind of breakdown. Consider the person whose personal life is still a mess because he has not yet effected inner healing, not yet translated what he has learned about his own personal history, his own brokenness, his own habitual misconceptions and self-delusions, into a healthier way of making choices in life. What will happen if that person takes a "leadership seminar" and learns all kinds of tactical maneuvers designed to help him become a "better leader"? Will some of those tactics stick? Sure. Will there be some surface change in the results this person will be able to deliver? Maybe. But over the long haul, this person will eventually falter and stumble and stall. Why? Because there is no "there" there. There is no purpose at the center of his life.

When you effect inner healing, you create a strong purpose, a strong sense of your mission in life, and you place that at the center of your experience. Then you can truly become the leader in your own life. This is a vitally important phase of growth for anyone and everyone who finds themselves coping with past trauma, anyone facing challenges in supporting their own growth and development because they've bought into coping rituals and survival techniques that don't really support them. And let's face it: That is pretty much all of us.

HOW CAN YOU TELL IF YOU HAVE BEGUN TO EFFECT INNER HEALING IN YOUR LIFE?

It's not uncommon for people to ask me how they can be certain they have at least *begun* the process of effecting inner healing. They understand and accept what I tell them about creating a sense of purpose, a sense of mission, a sense of responsibility for accepting the role of leadership in one's own life. They also understand this is an ongoing activity, something to which they must be ready, willing, and able to return on a regular basis—as opposed to something they can check off a list and consider themselves as having "arrived." Yet they want to know: How will I be able to tell I am on the right path with this? How can I be certain I've actually reached this point in my life, in my interactions with others, and in my relationship with my partner?

The answer here is pretty straightforward, and it surprises some people: Emotional intimacy will make a comeback in your life together.

When you have both been working the Process, and you are both fully supportive of the work you are doing and both fully committed to doing what is necessary to put what you know into practice, you will reach this step. One of you may reach it a little earlier than the other, but with the support and encouragement of your mentor, you will eventually both reach it, and as a result you will both begin to experience authentic emotional intimacy.

THE SECOND PHASE OF CONNECTEDNESS

A common question I hear when I point this out is, "Once we get to this step, will we feel the same kind of connectedness we felt when we were first falling in love?" And the answer I have to that is: "No. It will be even better."

Of course, it's understandable to want to recapture that intense connection you felt in the early, courtship phase of your relationship. But is it really possible to maintain that forever? The grown-up answer is no, because that was a different time in each of your lives. But don't let that reality get you down: There is a powerful positive side to this. Your level of connectedness and emotional intimacy can now become far deeper, far more meaningful, and, yes, even more romantic than it was in the early days. As special as that time was, we need to recognize that one of the reasons we may get nostalgic about the courtship period is that it was warm, fuzzy, and, above all, easy. That kind of closeness is wonderful—but the closeness you experience from effecting inner healing is the real thing.

This is the stuff that lasts, and it is even better than your courtship was. This is what you have both been working together to build. Think about it: Would you really want to go back to the beginning, and undo everything you have learned in the interim about yourselves, each other, and what it takes to sustain and grow your relationship? **Don't waste time wishing you could go back to the beginning. Moving forward is much better.**

Together, you will begin creating a second and far deeper phase of emotional intimacy—a feeling of profound security and comfort in the intimate presence of the person you love, and a closeness rooted in a deep understanding and acceptance of who you truly are and who the other person truly is. This is one of the most inspiring and powerful benchmarks of the Process, one that I have seen emerge countless times: Partners begin to trust each other again and confide in each other again. And unlike the rush of intimacy that occurs in the courtship phase, this reopening of intimacy is fueled by something that may not have been there during the earliest phase of your relationship: awareness of the other person's temperament, strengths, weaknesses, and personal history. This, in short, is real intimacy. It is what makes physical intimacy worth sharing— and rewarding on a deeply personal (not just physical) level when it is shared. This powerful second phase of intimacy is what happens when you commit to working through the Process together, and follow through on that commitment, under the guidance of a mentor.

CULTIVATION MEANS TAKING ACTION

None of us can feel safe in an intimate relationship by ourselves. To build an emotional safety zone in our intimate relationship with our partner—a zone that makes it safe to express how we feel and is sustainable over time—we need to understand that this kind of safety is the result of cultivation. It does not happen by accident. It happens because we have followed the steps and made a conscious, coordinated series of decisions that point us toward a deeper and deeper understanding of our true self and the true self of our partner. The emergence of such a safety zone is the fruit of our initial emotional healing—the reward, if you will, for all the hard work we have put in up to this point. But it is more than that: it is an essential prerequisite for *ongoing* healing, both as a couple and at the level of the individual.

Every intimate partnership needs such a safety zone if it is to survive as a viable covenant between two trusting, vulnerable, imperfect human beings who have committed their lives to one another.

What the Process has taught me, both as a husband and as a mentor, is that two people can—with a mutual understanding and acceptance of the stakes involved, and a mutual commitment to fulfill important agreements—*create or recreate* that safety zone even after it may have appeared to be obliterated forever. **Even after a crisis or a series of crises—adultery, substance abuse, financial collapse, you name it—you and your partner can rediscover emotional intimacy, or perhaps discover it for the first time.** It may not be easy. It may require taking actions you didn't expect to take. But it can be done. And the way to make it happen is cultivation. That means taking action. It means changing what you are doing now.

Effecting inner healing does not happen if you keep holding on tight to the status quo with both hands. But if you work the Process, if you accept the coaching that is central to it, if you make constructive changes, you will see the emotional safety zone beginning to widen, and you will eventually see it reclaim its rightful place at the center of your life. This fifth step is where that happens. For most of the couples I work with, this is nothing short of a miracle. It is also a cause of hope—something many couples have not felt for some time. Yet I must emphasize again and again with the couples I work with that this kind of hope, this feeling that progress is not just possible but present in our lives, is not mere optimism. It is the result of actions and decisions—notably the decision to work with a mentor and take on board that mentor's considered recommendations about how best to establish new patterns of thought and behavior that support the couple.

Some of these recommendations will be relatively easy to implement. Others may seem unfamiliar or even threatening at first, Examples include: reading certain books and articles together; taking part in vulnerable discussions; spending prayerful time together; and scheduling structured "couple time" even though one or both parties may have come to value the "freedom" they associate with being able to rely on some familiar routine of self-absorption.

For the record, watching television together definitely qualifies as a familiar routine of self-absorption—and so does an addiction to checking one's phone. **Excessive "screen time" is a major obstacle to establishing intimacy in a relationship.** In my work, one of the biggest challenges that spouses face is the issue of what to do when the other person is on the phone all the time. We may not realize it, but this choice to "just check the phone" for long periods of time sends a powerful negative message to our partner, a message that can quickly undermine any progress we may have made in creating an emotional safety zone.

When we pick up our phone and tune out our partner we send the message there are other things "out there" that are more important, more interesting, more fulfilling, and more (fill in the blank with whatever you feel most insecure about). The biggest problem with what I call "checking my phone syndrome" is that it quickly destroys any emotional intimacy the couple may have built up together—something that's already difficult enough to cultivate. As a mentor, I am constantly advising people to take one simple step that will expand the safety zone and save their marriage: Set aside part of the day that isn't "screen time," but rather "couple time."

Some of the most sensitive discussions with the mentor in support of effecting inner healing may involve challenging a couple's working assumptions about sexuality. If the couple have initiated a sexually intimate relationship before formalizing a legal marriage commitment, the mentor may recommend that they sign a Purity Covenant, under which both partners agree to embrace abstinence until they are actually married. Many people push back forcefully against the advice to sign such an agreement . . . but the reality, confirmed in countless cases, is that this kind of covenant can and does improve emotional intimacy. It makes healing possible in a relationship that would otherwise be doomed. Whenever a mentor makes a recommendation that changes the couple's current (dysfunctional) pattern of interaction, he or she does so with the clear goal of ensuring that the step of effecting inner healing can take root. The mentor knows full well that, in many cases, if there are not significant changes in lifestyle and behavior the safety zone will collapse. Emotional intimacy will continue to diminish or disappear entirely.

JERRY AND DIANNE

One classic dysfunctional pattern is the cycle of using so-called "makeup sex" as a replacement for the emotional intimacy that once existed in the relationship but has since vanished. One couple I worked with, Jerry and Dianne, actually perpetuated a cycle of constant conflict simply to get to the point where they could have emotionally distant sex with one another following the latest argument! (Jerry and Dianne are not yet married.) Dianne told me at one point, "I don't even know him anymore. I know this sucks." She knew the cycle was an unhealthy one, and she was desperately unhappy with the state of their relationship. Jerry was miserable as well. Neither of them knew what to do about it.

I pointed out that this emotionally bankrupt arrangement was only going to get worse for both of them. I warned them **"This sucks" could very easily move into "This sucks so bad that I'm leaving" or "This sucks so bad that I need to go somewhere else to get my needs met."**

I made the case, over and over again, that they had reached the point in the Process where their decisions, their *actions,* needed to align with what they knew about themselves if they truly wanted to move forward.

Their story serves as a perfect example of a situation where premature physical intimacy served as a significant obstacle to a healthy relationship. It's also a great example of the transformative power of a Purity Covenant. When I first raised the possibility of Jerry and Dianne reclaiming intimacy in their relationship by pledging to observe abstinence until they reached a point where they could make the commitment of getting married, they really didn't want to hear about it. But I kept bringing it up. A big part of the job of being a mentor is being persistent, being willing to say something people don't necessarily want to hear.

Eventually they both acknowledged that something big had to change, that they had to move past what was familiar but dysfunctional and had to focus instead on what was best for the relationship. They signed the Covenant. And they honored it. It took a while for emotional healing to begin. Dianne simply shut down for a long period of time when she was confronted with the challenge of dealing with the pain of her past. But Jerry kept working with me, and eventually Dianne came around and decided to follow through. Many times when we are confronted with this type of a challenge it takes a while for us to decide to "go there" because of the fear of what's going to be found as a result of the excavation of one's past history. The mentor's job is to keep pointing toward the path that leads to healing, no matter how long it may take for both partners to come around. Jerry kept persevering, despite Dianne's absence, and kept working on himself, which served as a statement to her of the level of his commitment to her. This kind of perseverance is a key determinant of a couple's success with the Process.

JACK AND CAROL

Married couples, of course, may also find themselves holding on tightly to a status quo that simply isn't working. Jack and Carol had been married for more than a decade. They seemed locked in a constant pattern of bitterness, recrimination, and blaming each other—a pattern that was so intense and so deeply ingrained it appeared to make emotional intimacy an impossibility. Their cutting exchanges in their first session with me were so unforgiving, so harsh, and so vicious I remember thinking something that I very rarely think when I talk to a couple for the first time: "If I were a betting man, I would not bet on these two being able to stay together for long."

Despite such dark presentiments on my side, though, Jack and Carol both insisted that they wanted to work through the Process, and they were both firm in their commitment to turn things around and save their marriage. With that strong commitment in place, they agreed to begin their one-on-one sessions with me, and I agreed to work with each of them independently.

The heavy lifting began. Each of them worked through the first four steps of the Process, and each of them learned a great deal along the way. Several months in, a real moment of truth came along for Jack. I asked him to make the effecting inner healing step a reality in his life by taking action to change a specific pattern of behavior, one that he acknowledged was a major obstacle to intimacy in his marriage: his severe addiction to online pornography.

Jack and I had been talking about this problem for weeks. He knew it was something that was standing in the way of his efforts to reconnect with Carol . . . and he knew she knew that too. He regarded the problem as something he had to change in his life. But he kept slipping. He had made any number of good-faith efforts on his own to disengage from this addiction, and I had done my best to support him in those efforts—but like other addictions that carry the potential to ensnare people, cancel the possibility of emotional intimacy, and wreck relationships, this one was one that could not be overcome without the help of a trained professional.

I suggested Jack take part in a twelve-week online counseling program I had found, led by Pure Life Ministries, that was specifically designed to provide spiritual, social, and therapeutic support to men in his situation. By taking part in this program, he would not only get access to tactics that have proven successful for others, and professional help in combating his addiction, but also receive peer reinforcement from other men facing the same problem he was. **Peer support can make all the difference in the world to someone struggling with a serious addiction.**

After thinking it over and discussing it with Carol, Jack agreed to take part in the program. He had relapses over the course of that twelve weeks, but he eventually completed the program successfully. The experience was transformative. Jack overcame his addiction, and he has continued to make life without pornography a reality in his daily life. This was a breakthrough moment in their work with me, and in their marriage. Jack's willingness to put in the (significant) time, effort, and energy to overcome this addiction and make his relationship with Carol the priority changed this couple from one I thought might not make it to one that I would be proud to hold up as an example of what following the Process can achieve.

Jack was proud of what he had accomplished, too, and he certainly had a right to be. He had made effecting inner healing a reality for himself . . . and for Carol. All of this has exposed areas of deep brokenness in each of their sexual histories, topics they had not explored together completely and that they will need to work through with a qualified specialist. They each have a long way to go to complete the excavation of their personal history. What I want you to notice, though, is that they're still working the Process, and as a result, they have definitely reestablished emotional intimacy in their lives, which is quite an accomplishment. Carol told me: "Sometimes I still can't believe it. I really didn't think it was possible. I got my husband back. He's free now, and we are connected again." The Process is what allowed them to get to a point where they could directly address important issues about intimacy that had been buried for many years.

MOVING BEYOND CRISIS-TO-CRISIS MODE

In both of the cases I just shared with you—Jerry and Dianne making justifications for a lifestyle built around premarital sex, and Jack and Carol trying to navigate an intimacy crisis that was being steadily worsened by an online addiction—denial about what was really happening only made things worse. **Denial and effecting inner healing cannot coexist.** Going into denial about the areas in our lives where we are making choices that lead us to disconnect ourselves from the person we are meant to be, or minimizing the importance of changing those choices, leads inevitably to a certain kind of pattern in the relationship. I call it living "crisis to crisis." This is classic coping and hoping behavior.

In relationships where denial about what's really going on is strong in one or both partners, there is a deep lack of emotional intimacy and safety. This leads to a downward cycle of poor communication, people taking things the wrong way, unsuccessful efforts to read the other person's mind, and a steadily accumulating inventory of resentment. This is what happens when people do not or cannot trust in the love of their partner: they experience crisis after crisis, argument after argument, misunderstanding after misunderstanding, escalation after escalation. These crises are not directly connected to any *external* crisis of the kind that everyone eventually has to deal with (such as the death of a parent.) They are predictable behavioral patterns within the relationship. Crisis to crisis was the pattern that both of these couples found themselves living. All four of them eventually came to the conclusion that crisis to crisis was no way to live. And all four of them were right. This is not the way any of us are meant to live. This pattern of behavior can easily spawn codependency patterns, counter dependency issues, and other serious problems.

When you finally move out of denial and change the behaviors standing in the way of effecting inner healing, you make emotional intimacy possible in your relationship. You then begin to build up deeper and deeper levels of trust with your partner, and vice versa. At that point something remarkable happens: the crises abate. Once you reach a place where you have deep trust in the love of the other person, you don't immediately get offended by what they do or say. You don't look for reasons to confirm your deepest doubts about them. **The fifth step of the process is where you take *action* to make the critical transition from denial to trust, from distance to intimacy, under the guidance of the mentor.**

REACHING THE SAFETY ZONE MEANS GOING OUTSIDE OF THE COMFORT ZONE

When I reach this all-important point of *action* with a couple I'm working with as a mentor, I sometimes have to remind them, gently, that they're not doing this for me. I am not telling them what to do. I am not trying to impose any kind of judgment on their lives. I am simply pointing out that by sticking with patterns of behavior that are familiar but dysfunctional they are making it impossible to create true emotional intimacy in their relationship. If they are serious about building up a safety zone of trust and mutual support within that relationship, *they* must make the choices necessary to go outside of the current comfort zone and establish a new way of taking action—and they must take action for *their* own reasons, not mine. They have to assign value to their own actions, and they have to choose to act. I can't do it for them. No mentor can.

During my initial meetings with a couple, I will ask people to describe their purpose in life. Many will say things like, "I want to fulfill God's purpose for me and do what God wants." This often leads to an interesting conversation. If they are serious about fulfilling God's purpose for them, how does that purpose extend to activities like looking at pornography or having premarital sex?

When I ask tough questions like that, I am not trying to tell anyone what to do. I am not attempting to impose some legalistic religious judgment. I am, however, pointing out a disconnect between the stated purpose and the actions that are taking place within the relationship. If they want to experience the benefit of emotional connection and deep support from the other person, they need to take a close look at whether their actions are supporting that goal and their stated purpose. If they want a different outcome, they must be willing to take different actions. The path to accepting this reality may be long or it may be short—but it is one couples who are successful in their execution of the Process always end up following.

Let me be very clear: In order to make emotional healing a reality in your life, in order to support you as you begin to move out of the realm of theory and into the world of action, your mentor is going to ask you to consider doing things that don't feel comfortable, familiar, or "normal" to you (at least as far as contemporary culture defines the word "normal"). **Your mentor is going to keep raising the possibility of you going outside of your comfort zone in order to create the safety zone.** And your first response may be to ignore or minimize that advice. Even if you are resistant initially, you will serve yourself, your partner, and your relationship most fully if you keep listening and keep looking for ways to follow the Process.

At first, Dianne and Jerry were deeply resistant to the whole idea of taking pen in hand and signing a commitment that reads in part, "In obedience to God's command, I promise to protect your sexual purity from this day until our honeymoon." You may be resistant to it, too, if you are unmarried and sexually active with your partner. But you know what? For Dianne and Jerry, making and keeping that pledge, with the guidance and support of a mentor, turned out to be an essential prerequisite to their personal experience of the step of effecting inner healing. It may just turn out to be that way for you, too.

STUDY QUESTIONS

Have you ever been in a situation where something that seemed like a major weakness on your part connected to a major strength in another situation? For instance, has the trait "stubbornness" also manifested itself as "persistence"? Make a list of as many such paired traits as you can think of and write down as much as you can about each situation.

What would you say is your greatest weakness? How could that be transformed into a strength?

Why is personal accountability important in personal relationships?

Are there any areas in your relationship where you are tempted to blame your partner for the state of the relationship? In what specific areas would your partner say you are most inclined to cast blame on him or her?

Based on what you have learned so far about the steps of the Process, how can you see them helping you when it comes to taking personal responsibility and making better choices?

One of the hallmarks of the effecting inner healing step is that it results in better choices—choices that support your relationship over the long term. What choices have you made over the past six months that did not take the relationship in the direction you wanted it to go? What better choices could you have made? Be as detailed in your written response to this question as possible.

Our decisions don't just affect us. They also affect the people in our lives. What are some examples of decisions you made without fully realizing how they would affect your partner? Identify at least three from the past six months. Explain each situation in depth, and the decision you wish you had made instead.

What does "loving every version of yourself" mean to you? What's an example of a time when you found it difficult to love every version of yourself? What would have to happen for you to be able to love every version of yourself?

What was a time in your life when you decided you valued yourself enough to take on coaching from someone else and to make an investment of time, attention, or money that would bring about transformation? If you were willing to make that kind of change in your career or your company, are you willing to make it on behalf of your relationship? Why or why not?

What are three patterns of behavior you personally engage in that need to change in to better support your relationship with your partner? Why do they need to change?

What does compassion mean to you? When did you last show compassion to your partner? Is it possible to be compassionate with yourself? Explain your answer.

Often, we fall into the trap of defining ourselves by means of our job title or what we believe we have accomplished, as opposed to what we believe in or what we are committed to. With this in mind, how would you answer the question "Who are you?"

Have you ever prioritized goals related to social status, career advancement, or financial gain over goals related to addressing challenges in your personal life? If so, what is an example of that? What was the effect of this set of priorities on your relationship with your partner? What would your partner say the effect will be five years from now if this pattern continues?

Do you ever feel nostalgic for the early dating or "courtship" phase of your relationship? If so, is it possible that what you miss sometimes is the fact that it was easier to be together back then? What could you do to build a new phase of your relationship that is even richer and deeper than your early phase was?

Have any of your personal relationships been based all or nearly all on sexuality and physical attraction? Explain your answer.

Will sexuality alone sustain a workable relationship over the long term? Why or why not?

Is emotional intimacy the same thing as physical intimacy? Explain your answer.

How can you work together to create a larger, more protective zone of emotional safety for yourself and your partner? What behavioral changes would have to take place on your side? How could a mentor help you develop the resilience and perseverance necessary to make those behavioral changes?

"Screen time" is a major contemporary challenge to the cultivation of couple intimacy. Are you willing to prioritize your relationship ahead of screen time? Why or why not? Could changing your priorities in this area affect your relationship in a positive way? How?

What other priorities would you have to change to create a deeper level of emotional connection with your partner, a connection that goes beyond status quo living?

What areas in your current relationship have you avoided discussing with your partner because raising the issue felt too uncomfortable? Why did it feel uncomfortable?

Addictive behaviors come in many forms. Are you willing to uncover and deal with addictive behaviors and coping mechanisms that are preventing you from moving forward in your life? What are some of those behaviors?

What are some examples of areas in your life where you are moving from crisis to crisis with your partner?

What are some examples of areas in your life where you and/or your partner are in denial about the true nature of the challenges you face?

What are some examples of areas in your life where you and/or your partner are "coping and hoping"?

We often hold on to dysfunctional behaviors that are familiar to us and that have become part of our comfort zone—isolation, for instance, or avoiding crucial conversations, or spending long hours on the phone. What are three behavior patterns in your life that are familiar but unsupportive of the relationship?

9
Maintaining New Found Disciplines

WHEN PEOPLE BEGIN the Process, they are a little bit like a driver attempting to drive from the back seat of a car with the two front wheels removed. They can't see very well, they don't have a clear sense of where the car is going, they've got only a distant and tenuous grasp on the steering wheel, and they're in a vehicle being powered entirely by the two rear wheels: feelings and physiology. The journey they undertake is inevitably an unpredictable one, and it's often frightening. They may even get into an accident.

By the time they reach the fifth step, effecting inner healing, they've figured out—with the ongoing help and support of their mentor—that the vision is much better from the front seat, which is where they've now started sitting. They've got a better sense of where they actually want to go once they start the engine. As the engine hums, they've got both hands on the steering wheel.

And they've fixed the problem of the missing front wheels. They're now driving a car powered, as it's designed to be powered, by the two front wheels: authentic self and purpose. These are all things to celebrate.

But they don't yet have a license, because they haven't yet made the right habits second nature.

The sixth step of the Process is all about getting into the habit of getting into the front seat of the car and driving under the guiding power of the two front wheels—not just once in a while, but every single time. Not just when we are driving somewhere important, but any and every time we choose to drive anywhere. Not in order to make the mentor happy, or to win the mentor's approval, or to keep hearing the mentor's opinions and insights about what the best drivers do, but because it is both irresponsible and unsafe to attempt to drive the car in any other way.

It is worth pointing out that we don't refer to the sixth step of the Process as the "final" step. There is nothing final about it. Under the mentor's guidance, both partners in the relationship are now recapping and reexperiencing certain earlier steps as often and as deeply as necessary, so as to make them second nature—a matter of personal discipline and personal habit. The mentor is shining a spotlight on those areas where work still remains to be done. We may find that forgiveness is incomplete in certain corners of our life. We may discover there are certain assumptions and preconceptions in our thought life that are not supporting us. We may find there are patterns of behavior that are keeping us or our partner from experiencing the inner healing we both need. Here in the sixth step, the mentor is going to help us identify where there is work that still needs to be done in fulfilling and living those earlier steps, making choices that support our authentic selves *as a matter of personal discipline.*

"Do not lie to each other, since you have taken off your old self with its practices and have put on the new self, which is being renewed in knowledge in the image of its Creator" (Colossians 3:9–10, NIV)

Every action the mentor has undertaken up to this point has been leading toward this critical sixth step, the step of establishing and sustaining internal transformations that result in new disciplines in everyday life. The aim of the mentor, after all, is to help the couple learn to align themselves and their marriage, as a matter of habit, with the will of God . . . *not* with the will of the mentor.

TWO KINDS OF ACCOUNTABILITY

One of the most powerful tools for making that happen is accountability. But note there are two kinds of accountability in play here, and we need them both.

So say, for instance, the mentor passes along a suggestion during a session with a couple who is working the Process that they cut down on screen time in the time they spend together at home. He asks that they refrain from using their phones for anything other than answering or placing important calls between the hours of 6:00 p.m. and 10:00 p.m., four nights a week, and make a conscious effort to spend more of this time interacting with each other. The couple agrees to give this a try.

So what happens? The next week, they prepare to check in with the mentor, knowing one of the things they will need to discuss during the session is how well they did with this assignment. Notice that the knowledge that they eventually have to check back in with the mentor is, at least at first, the couple's most powerful incentive to complete the assignment. They don't want to be seen by the mentor as not following through on something important. If they didn't have the next session scheduled with the mentor, or if that session were cancelled, they might well forget about the assignment. External accountability, up to this point, has been among the most powerful incentives for them to take action and change the status quo.

But external accountability is not enough. Here in the sixth step, the mentor's goal is going to be to get them to begin taking such steps in support of the relationship—*not* because the mentor said to do it, but because both people in the relationship know that minimizing screen time and spending more time interacting with each other face-to-face is part of who they are as individuals, part of the couple they are committed to becoming. They learn to do it on their own, and they do it as a matter of course, because they are now *internally* accountable. When external accountability gives way to internal accountability, on a small scale or a large scale, the mentor has succeeded, at least in part, in doing the job.

External accountability makes newfound disciplines familiar. Internal accountability makes them sustainable. Without internal accountability, the sixth step is incomplete. You don't want to have the driving instructor constantly *remind* you that the best way to drive a car is get in on the driver's side at the front of the vehicle and place your hands firmly on the steering wheel once you've started the engine.

You want to do those things as a matter of course, because doing them is an important part of taking on the personal responsibility of driving a car in the first place!

THE PARADOX OF THE SIXTH STEP

Maintaining newfound disciplines is, at the end of the day, not merely an emotional change but a spiritual change as well—a change so profound that to be sustainable it requires what I can only describe as a spiritual transformation. What I mean by this is that the kind of transformative personal change we are talking about here requires an ongoing connection with our Creator as a source of personal power, so we can move past our dysfunctional, habitual learned defenses—some of which are very deeply ingrained indeed—and replace them with new patterns of behavior that support us. In my own experience, this transformation is simply impossible without Divine support. And yet I have worked with countless people who explicitly rejected any aspect of spiritual life—people who rejected belief in scripture, belief in

God, belief in an afterlife—who not only reached this step, but made it an important part of their lives, their intimate relationships, and their interactions in the workplace. How can we explain this?

The answer, I believe, is to be found in the powerful, approachable word "purpose."

Very often, we sabotage any practical expression of spirituality by insisting on placing our own words on what is happening. For me, the sustaining force that creates momentum in maintaining newfound disciplines is best described as Divine . . . a relational experience with God, just as it is a relational experience with a partner.

As I make a habit of pointing out to each and every person I serve as mentor, **the Process is pragmatic.** It is based on you taking what works and using it. Nowhere is that more true than here in the sixth step. It is likely there are going to be moments when what the mentor shares with you about maintaining newfound disciplines ends up connecting with a spiritual concept. The advice I shared with you earlier in this book is more relevant than ever here! If that spiritual connection doesn't make sense for you right now, that's OK . . . it will come.

This next part comes as a surprise to some people who are used to thinking of me as a Christian minister (which I certainly am). As a minister, the quality of my own relationship to God matters deeply to me. But as a mentor, my job is to help you maintain the disciplines that support your true self and your ability to express yourself and be compassionate toward others. **If you don't believe in God, my job as mentor does not change.** If you have no idea how to even approach the question of the Divine in your life, my job description remains exactly the same as when I am working with someone who operates within my own belief system. When it comes to supporting you and helping you move from external accountability to internal accountability, what matters is my ability to help you begin to address certain essential, inescapable facts of human life.

These facts include:

- At some point in your development, you have faced challenges, and perhaps trauma, that has left your wounded self (also known as your ego) in a position where your habitual responses to situations are often triggered by fear, insecurity, and a deep instinct to protect yourself at any cost—even when doing so perpetuates brokenness and dysfunction.

- The good news is that these protective instincts, even the most dysfunctional ones, have supported your efforts to survive up to this point in your life.
- The bad news is that these protective instincts are deeply destructive of your efforts to awaken your true self and bring it to a position of prominence that supports your most important relationships.
- The pattern of your responses has to change and the change has to be sustainable for you to emerge as the leader in your own life.
- You must be able to turn to a source of enduring power within yourself if you wish to learn to not react instinctively with your learned defenses and if you wish to learn to make compassion toward yourself and others the new normal—even when the feelings are painful and the temptation to indulge old patterns of behavior seems overwhelming.
- Our own "power", our own way, is what gets us into trouble, along with our unhealthy choices, and reactions to our brokenness. When we discover the "power" of the Divine nature available to us, we can begin to rely on that power, not our own.
- This source of enduring power within yourself will help you define your PURPOSE. **Your purpose is the reason you are here on earth.**
- The more you practice staying connected to this source of enduring power within yourself, and the better you get at using it to maintain the newfound disciplines that support you, the safer you will feel internally, the better you will be at expressing your own feelings and understanding the feelings of others, and the more your relationships will improve.

The purpose of life is not to be happy. It is to be useful, to be honorable, to be compassionate, to have it make some difference that you have lived and lived well.
— Ralph Waldo Emerson

ADAM AND EDDY

One of the most inspiring couples I have ever had the privilege of working with—a couple who has put these principles to work, been persistent, and seen positive results from each step of the Process up to and including the sixth step—is Adam and Eddy. Eddy is a believer, Adam is not. Think of how easy it would have been for me as their mentor to create barriers to them making progress in deepening their relationship by assuming that I was dealing with two Christians. I wasn't!

I was (and am) sensitive to the reality that many people from the LGBTQ+ Community have strong negative associations with organized religion as a whole. Why? They have been bombarded with threatening, uncompassionate, and judgmental messaging about their sexuality from any number of people in their lives claiming to speak on behalf of God. So, I left Adam plenty of space to consume as much or as little of what I was offering as he saw fit. He is a classic example of someone who stayed with the Process, not because of its spiritual resonances but because of a pragmatic and steadily stronger belief in its ability to heal and sustain his marriage.

Adam said:

> *I was never openly resistant to working with Bill, but it is certainly true that in the early days it was not a high priority for me, and I didn't understand how much of a priority it was for Eddy. He was the one who really wanted to pursue working with Bill. The whole reason I eventually agreed to work with Bill, and have continued to work with him, had nothing to do with any spiritual or religious*

beliefs on my side. It had everything to do with the fact that we had reached a point in our relationship where we both acknowledged we could benefit from the support of a professional. I only reached that point when Eddy told me that he was seriously thinking about leaving me. Taking part in the Process was the alternative to that. So I made it a priority, and I'm glad I did. Looking back, it probably took longer than it should have. I eventually came to see how the sessions with Bill could help us to grow as individuals and to become better partners. And over the past year and a half, that is what we have experienced. Now we see him on average once a month.

Eddy's description of his experience of the Process shines a spotlight on the step of maintaining newfound disciplines. In the quote below, notice how Eddy has moved closer to a state of internal accountability for understanding and managing his own emotional responses to the situations he encounters in his relationship:

I don't like to say it was an ultimatum that I gave Adam about beginning to work with Bill. I would say, though, that it became obvious to me that we had gotten as far as we could get in fixing things on our own, based on what we knew. We had come to a point where we had to admit that we needed help from a professional, and we needed to trust Bill, who had come highly recommended to us. Trust has never been an easy thing for me, and trusting that someone could help us was a big step for me. I had the choice to walk away or to fight through and to try to fix the problems in our relationship, and I felt like I was ready to fight. The easiest route was to leave. The much harder path was to confront myself, to confront the long list of things I didn't understand about myself that was contributing to us getting so close to the breaking point.

My temperament connects strongly to the Choleric, and in my case that meant I was used to barging my way through situations so I could get what I wanted. Very often, I'll just blast everything out of the way and keep moving ahead. There were things I did that I thought were strong suits, things that I took pride in because my perception was that they had helped me to rise to a position of leadership very quickly. What I didn't realize, though, was how some of the same qualities were destroying important relationships along the way, including my relationship with my husband. I was pressuring and manipulating people into doing what I wanted. Getting a clearer sense of my temperament brought that into focus for me and helped me to see that I had some natural tendencies that weren't always serving my relationships. I had to learn to recognize those weaknesses and see if I could translate them into strengths. In order to do that, I had to face the truth about who I was and what my natural inclinations really were. That wasn't someone else barging my way through people. It was me.

Another area where I had to learn to take a close look at the truth was understanding how what had happened to me as a child affected my adult relationships. There was past trauma in my younger life. I was sexually abused at the age of five by someone I trusted. That experience led me to block people and push everybody away. Bill connected me with a therapist who specialized in helping people with experiences like mine. He also pointed out that my reactions to that trauma explained why I felt so empty, why I was pushing everyone in my life away, why I was pushing God away. At one point, he said, "No wonder you feel empty!" I realized that he was right.

That emptiness and that desire to push people away

didn't just come out of nowhere. It came out of my reaction to trauma.

The big transition for me when it comes to working the Process has been moving out of the mindset of doing this in order to fix a specific problem, and into the mindset of doing this to get a better understanding of myself. *At first, my attitude was that I was dealing with a hurricane. When you're in the middle of a hurricane, what you think about is, oh my God, how do I get out of the storm. You kind of go from crisis to crisis. And you want to solve the latest crisis. It's not like that anymore.*

For me the biggest difference was moving out of the mode that says "How do I survive this storm?" and into the mode that says, "I am doing this so that I can get a deeper understanding of myself and how I contribute to certain things," as opposed to constantly falling into emotional storms. I am no longer just focusing on the storm and talking about that and walking away, and then coming back a couple of weeks later to talk about another hurricane. I am figuring out how my decisions affect what I am experiencing.

I loved what Bill said to me once, which was that you need to identify what the button that causes the emotional storm is, and what that button is connected to. Where does the cable lead to? That was so powerful for me, because suddenly it wasn't about figuring out who's pressing that button so that I can make them stop doing that. Rather, I need to identify what that button is connected to so I can unplug it and disconnect it. That to me has become what I've been working on, which has allowed me to reach a place where I don't give so much power to other people. I'm not coming to Bill and saying I am in the middle of a storm, I need your help. It's much more about identifying patterns in myself. There are a lot of buttons that, with Bill's help and the help of the therapist he pointed me toward, I've figured out the wiring for, buttons that I've been able to disconnect. And there are some buttons I'm still working on. So that's the kind of thing that we keep coming back to Bill to talk about.

THE OTHER END OF THE SPECTRUM

In sharp contrast to the situation of ongoing, mutually supported personal growth Adam and Eddy have created in their lives is the situation of Gerald and Julianne.

They had made great progress during the year and a half that we had had monthly calls. I felt they had each reached a point where they understood their own temperament and had gotten a handle on self-assessment through journaling, had made forgiveness and releasing of judgment a reality in some of the most critical areas of their lives, had become more present in their own thought life by taking thoughts captive, and had begun to effect inner healing by changing behaviors that did not support them as individuals or as partners in a relationship. What I was not altogether certain of was whether they had reached a point in their marriage where they had transformed *external* accountability for sustaining and expanding all this hard work (i.e., accountability to me as their coach) to *internal* accountability (i.e., accountability to themselves as individuals).

In short, I had doubts about whether they had reached the step of maintaining newfound disciplines. I shared my concerns with them—tactfully, but directly. Both of them, but primarily Gerald, felt strongly about "moving on." **A desire to "just move on" is often a sign that someone is viewing the Process as something to be completed and checked off a list.** As I hope I've made clear by now, that's the exact opposite of the thinking and action that gets someone to the point where they can fulfill the sixth step.

I reached out to them and set up a check-in call, having not spoken to them for nearly eight months. Both of them were on the videoconference call at the same time. After exchanging a few pleasantries, we got down to the issue at hand, which was how things had been going in their marriage, and whether they had been able to sustain, or perhaps even expand, the progress they had made since we'd last spoken.

"How are you guys doing?" I asked.

Gerald jumped in first. (This was one of the patterns I had noticed in his communication; he liked to dominate discussions.) "Things have been great," he said. "It's much better than it was when we started with you. We're communicating better, we're dealing with conflict more effectively when it arises, and we're enjoying the time we spend together more than we did back when we first started the sessions. The work we did with you has really paid off, Bill." And Gerald went on to offer about five minutes' worth of nonstop enthusiasm about how great things were going in their relationship. I noticed that Julianne had been unable to get a word in edgewise and wasn't really trying to—a pattern we had identified, months earlier, as a sign of her being overwhelmed by Gerald's desire to dominate conversations.

When I asked Julianne to share how she felt things were going in the marriage, she was quiet and noncommittal. It seemed like she was just waiting for the call to be over. I pushed her just a little bit, gently assuring her that it was all right to share how she really felt, and that her willingness to do so had been one of the big reasons she and Gerald had been able to make such impressive strides in the months when we had been working together.

Julianne began to cry.

"This is what he does," she said, sobbing. "He jumps over everything. He doesn't care what I think, he speaks for both of us and makes decisions unilaterally, and pretends that's not what he's doing. It stopped for a while. It stopped when we were having monthly calls with you. I guess because he knew he was going to have to talk to you and be honest about what had happened since he last spoke to you.

But he got out of the habit of making an effort. And I got out of the habit of telling you what was going on."

The rest of the call was difficult. I explained to Gerald and Julianne that they had stopped reinforcing and maintaining newfound disciplines, because they hadn't made the transition to internal accountability. When they stopped the sessions, there was less and less effort to support and act on what they had learned about themselves and each other. Without me in the picture, things had gotten steadily worse, and they'd each found ways to distract themselves from that reality, or ignore it altogether.

Gerald was now trapped in the zone known as tolerable recovery: He kept falling back on the justification that they were better off than they were when they had first come to me, when their relationship was in deep crisis. Julianne was in coping-and-hoping mode: She kept struggling through, managing their familiar, steadily deepening problems as best she could, and hoping things would get better.

"Right now," I said, "you two guys are like the frog in the pan of water on the stove. The burner is on, and the water is getting slowly hotter, minute by minute. The frog never jumps out, because he doesn't realize the water is getting hotter, and so he boils to death. Gerald, you keep talking about how things are better than they were a year and a half ago. That may be true, but the way things are going, it won't be true for long. That water's going to reach the boiling point unless you both make the decision to reengage with the disciplines . . . and you reach a point where you're not relying on accountability to someone on the outside of the relationship in order to sustain change. I think you need to work the disciplines and make a couple of appointments to help you get this marriage back on track."

I'm not sure what they will ultimately decide. I know I gave them the steps to follow that would help them move forward on the sixth step.

THE SIXTH STEP IS ALL ABOUT CONTINUOUS FORWARD MOTION

In a marriage, you are either going forward or going backward. There is no standing still. If you've reached a point of stagnation, of stasis, of complacency, you might be tempted to imagine that you are standing still, and that that is good enough. For instance, you might be tempted to believe that the fact that the two of you are having fewer fights than you had back in the "bad old days" when the relationship was in imminent danger of collapse then the two of you must be on the right track. But you will be wrong. Not having as many fights may simply mean the two of you have gotten very good at avoiding conflict and pretending it doesn't matter if important issues aren't addressed. That is a recipe for collapse.

If you are not moving forward, if you are not consciously and continuously creating greater personal and spiritual intimacy in your lives together as a couple, you are losing ground. This is not about simply putting up with each other. You can live with someone and still wake up one morning and find that you have steadily been losing when it comes to creating a safety zone, an area of intimacy and trust in your marriage that you can both count on. That requires effort. It requires maintaining newfound disciplines that protect the intimacy and keep the relationship moving forward.

Many people convince themselves that they have made enough of an effort, and that they can just "settle in." Sadly, this is what most marriages look like in our time. Couples fool themselves into believing that living in the same place is the same thing as intimacy. It's not. There is a natural propensity for partners to drift apart in any relationship. If you don't make a conscious effort to counteract that drift, you follow it, and your relationship suffers as a result. This is what happens in the majority of marriages now, and it's the reason our divorce rate is so absurdly high: people grow used to "settling in," and they imagine that familiarity is the same thing as intimacy—until the marriage fails. That's because familiarity, on its own, tends to breed contempt.

Things we were once lovingly sensitive and attentive to can become annoyances, and without a deep connection to the other person, we may begin to nurse grudges.

Real intimacy, intimacy that grows and strengthens over time, gets you closer to the experience of being one with your partner. **You don't become one with someone just because you're living with them!**

The sixth step is all about maintaining forward momentum in your marriage by creating internal accountability and making it a reality in your life and in your marriage. That kind of accountability is the only thing that will sustain the hard-won progress made in the first five steps and extend that success into the long term. Yes, keeping this momentum going requires passion and commitment. It requires putting at least as much fire, love, time, passion, and creativity into knowing yourself and your partner as you do into other things . . . like doing your job, running your business, or catching up on your social media feed. But you *can* make your marriage a priority. And you might want to think about doing that, because **if your intimate life is in crisis, your business and your career are going to experience crises, as well.**

I can't tell you how many people I've met over the years who have chosen to put far more time, effort, energy, and attention into building and protecting their business than they have into building and protecting intimacy with their spouse. They set up a series of plans, backup plans, and backup plans for their business . . . but they won't put the same level of commitment into their marriage. They tell themselves, "We love each other. We will be OK." But loving each other is not enough. And eventually, if people "settle in" for long enough, two people who once loved each other find themselves far, far away from each other, and treating each other as adversaries.

The real enemy here is not your spouse. It is complacency. After five steps of the Process, you may come to believe that you have "fixed" the relationship, but the reality is that if you want it "fixed" in such a way that keeps it "fixed," you need personal disciplines in place that ensure that intimacy is real, meaningful, and growing steadily in your life together. With effort and support, the two of you can be among those who learn to create and sustain that kind of discipline without the ongoing help and support of a mentor. Once you reach that point of strong personal accountability on both sides of the marriage, you will have made the sacred, interconnected acts of both knowing and cultivating your true self—and growing closer to your spouse. Both acts are part of a lifelong Process of personal development. Both, I believe, support emotionally intelligent leadership in all aspects of your life.

STUDY QUESTIONS

Making decisions solely or mostly based on our feelings and our physiology is known as "driving from the back seat." Making decisions based on the strengths of our temperament and a rational assessment of the situation we face is known as "driving from the front seat." Which seat would you say that you typically drive from? Give an example that explains why you say that.

Accountability is important because it gives you the opportunity to make important decisions in consultation with others, including those who are likely to be affected by your decision. Has a lack of accountability ever resulted in choices on your part that didn't support your relationships? Give at least one example, explain what the lack of accountability looked like, and describe what an accountable course of action would have been.

What learned defenses, inherited from earlier periods of your life, do you instinctively employ in interactions with your spouse? (Example: Dominating a conversation so that others cannot express themselves.) Identify as many of these as you can.

For each learned defense you just identified, what would a more responsive and more vulnerable response look like?

What is the difference between surviving (moving from crisis to crisis) and thriving (creating forward movement) in your world? Describe an example of a time you were surviving, rather than thriving, in your relationship.

What's an example of a time when someone "pushed one of your buttons" and you reacted heedlessly or impulsively without understanding what was driving your reaction? Describe it in detail.

There's a saying: "Half measures avail us nothing." What's an example of a time when you felt you had taken meaningful steps to improve your relationship, but your partner felt very differently?

How has taking "half measures" led to a perpetuation of the cycle of tolerable recovery in your relationship?

Complacency is one of the biggest enemies of intimacy and good communication in a relationship. What are some specific examples of patterns of dysfunctional behavior on your part that you've grown used to, but that could threaten or ultimately kill your relationship?

What are some specific areas where you have taken your partner for granted?

The sixth step of the Process requires both self-awareness and accountability to oneself, as well as accountability to others, to ensure continuous forward movement and growth in the relationship. Of what kinds of emotional reactions to stress could you be more self-aware? To whom are you now accountable? Would that person agree that you are accountable to him or her? Why or why not?

Without engagement in a process that builds compassion, partners in a relationship can very easily drift toward resentment, grudges, and eventually contempt. What is an example of something your partner did early in the relationship that you once found endearing, but now find annoying? How would your partner answer this question?

Are you as passionate about making improvements in your relationship with your partner as you are your business, vocation, or career? Explain your answer. What answer would your partner give to this question?

10
The Three Big Misconceptions

NOW THAT WE have seen in depth what happens in the six steps of the Process, we need to devote some time to debunking the biggest misconceptions people tend to have about what we have covered. These misconceptions tend to arise when someone reaches a distant, preliminary level of understanding about what this work is all about but hasn't experienced it in person.

Reading about the Process is not the same as working the Process consistently in your own life. Until you begin to do that it is likely you will fall prey to one or all of the misconceptions addressed below. I've touched on each of them briefly in earlier sections, but they are worth examining a little more closely now so you have the context you need to make good decisions once you complete the book.

MISCONCEPTION NUMBER ONE: "THIS IS A CHECKLIST"

Most of us are used to thinking of "steps" as leading to some point of completion, some stage where we don't have to worry about the steps once we've checked them off a list. The Process is not like that. It's a way of life. Once you start this, you don't reach a point where you are done with all the steps. That's not how a relationship works, whether the relationship is between you and your spouse, you and a colleague, or you and God. **In a working relationship, you always keep moving forward, and you always keep looking for ways to improve the connection.**

Think about it. The whole purpose of the sixth step, maintaining newfound disciplines—which you just read about—is continuous self-examination and self-accountability. That means the Process doesn't stop.

It is an *ongoing* journey based on understanding and reinforcing *each* of the five steps that preceded it. **You will never be "done" with the six steps of the Process.** I have shared them with you sequentially because they tend to make the most sense when you learn about them in the order I've shared. They're easiest to implement when they make sense to you. But they are interdependent, and they are likely to require action and attention throughout your life. Embrace that.

Your mentor's job will not be to wave you off as you walk happily into the sunset, but to make sure you are prepared to take personal responsibility for creating the possibility of emotionally intelligent leadership in your intimate relationships—and in all your relationships. That is a lifetime commitment.

MISCONCEPTION #2: "I CAN DO THIS ON MY OWN"

The reality is, if we're talking about the entire Process, you can't. None of us can. **We each need a mentor in our lives to help us get a clear sense of who we really are, what our obstacles and our**

opportunities are, and what blind spots we need help learning to recognize and counteract.

I do realize it's entirely possible that you've come across some concepts and strategies in this book that have led you to think to yourself, "That's a pretty good idea. I should give that a try in our relationship." I'm happy that you've had that reaction, and I want nothing but the best for you and yours, and hope you do end up giving it a try. But I want you to give the *whole Process* a try, under the guidance of a mentor, for the simple reason that that's what works to turn people's lives around. It can turn your life around too.

MISCONCEPTION #3: "THIS IS JUST FOR COUPLES"

I mentioned very early in this book that **the Process is really for everyone—single, married, or "it's complicated."** The examples I've shared with you have involved married couples who work together, because that's who has benefited most from implementing the Process. But before you get to the Epilogue, where I'll share some final thoughts on what could happen next in your life, I want to point out that some of the most powerful testimonies the Process has generated has come from single people. Many of these were people who kept working the steps week after week, month after month, until they found the right partner, got the Partner to start working the steps, and eventually became part of a married couple whose relationship was grounded in the Process. One of my favorite testimonies was Mark's:

> When I began the journey with Bill, I really didn't have any idea of where I would end up. As a single man, bachelor, living on my own, there was a ton of "reformatting" that had to be done. He began to break down my temperaments and how I was allowing myself to be a victim of my natural tendencies, rather than be in control of my life—or should I say, rather than allowing God access to my life to

help give me self-control. The results of my choices before I started the Process were typical—continual failed relationships. Working with Bill shed light on this and allowed me to really buckle down and make the changes necessary to start to really make lasting improvements in my life. That was when God opened the door for me to meet my now wife, Christy-Ann.

As we started dating and getting more serious, I encouraged her to have a session with Bill. She began to dig into her own temperaments and learn about her own strengths and weaknesses. She entered the Process alongside me.

Bill was able to work with BOTH Christy-Ann and myself, as he had intimate knowledge of us individually, and then us as a couple. He was able to alert us of challenges we had brushed under the rug, and he helped us to avoid mistakes that could have been devastating. Through regular monthly meetings with Bill, separately and together, through conversations, reading, and "Billwork," we got to a point where we could confidently enter into marriage and begin to start a life together as one. Bill's premarital counseling was essential to us reaching that point in our lives.

We knew that was not the end of the story. Because we had worked so closely with Bill, we knew that the foundation of marriage begins at, well, the beginning. We dug further into our time with Bill, our reading, our conversations, and we continued to grow as a couple. Now we have been married over a year. We continue to regularly meet with Bill to learn more about ourselves both individually and as a couple, and to prepare ourselves for the next stages in our lives together. There is no sweeping things under the rug. There is no avoidance or pretending that everything is OK. Instead, our marriage is based facing everything head on and being properly equipped for the storms when they come. And instead of pretending to be OK, we know we can actually be vulnerable and authentic with each other—and make it through the storm.

Neither of us can even conceive of a relationship without the ongoing leadership and mentorship in our marriage that we have gotten by working the Process. We meet with Bill once a month and look forward to our continued journey to emotional and spiritual health in our marriage.

STUDY QUESTIONS

Are you willing to pursue the Process, not as a short-term "fix," but as a long-term change to the way you look at your life and your relationships?

Have you ever reached a point in your relationship where you said or thought, "I just want to move on"? If so, what problems or dysfunctional behavior patterns would remain if you did "move on"? What would you really be "moving on" to?

Are you skeptical about whether working with a mentor is right for you? Why or why not?

Have you been assuming up to this point that you can handle the challenges in your relationship on your own? What have the results been so far of you doing that?

What are the five most important relationships in your life, other than your relationship with your partner? Are there any patterns that you see in those relationships that mirror issues that exist in your relationship with your partner? If so, what are they?

Do you want to be part of a marriage that lasts? If so, what kinds of changes are going to have to happen?

Epilogue

In a marriage, you're never standing still. You're either moving forward or going backward. In other words, if your relationship is static, it's really degenerating. Now that you have reached the end of the book, I am hoping you can appreciate the value of initiating a relationship with a mentor who can support you and your partner as you begin to master the neglected art of deciding to move forward together . . . and learning what needs to happen for that movement to take place. This willingness to support mutual growth and progress in the relationship is the core prerequisite of the all-too-easily-neglected management skill known as "leading from home."

It's very common for people considering taking on the Process to ask me two questions that seem, at first, entirely reasonable:

- How much time will this take out of my working week?
- When will this be over?

Each of these questions reflects a fundamental misunderstanding about the Process, a misunderstanding about the nature of our intimate relationships as they affect our working lives. Before we close this book, I think it's important that we examine the misunderstandings connected to each question.

The unspoken subtext of the first question is, "I am a busy person, and I need to prioritize my time investments carefully, including the amount of time I invest in the Process." Very often, people will tell me that they don't have a lot of, or any, time to set aside for the Process. Whenever I hear this, I know with certainty that I am talking to someone who needs to start the Process sooner, rather than later.

You don't find the time to do the Process. You make the time. If you received a phone call telling you that your house was on fire, would you ask the person on the other end of the line to estimate how much time dealing with the fire was going to take? None of us have any extra time. But that doesn't stop us from finding ways to make our companies more effective and more competitive. Even though there is no available time, we make the time. If your intimate life is important to you, you will make the time for that, too. If you make the mistake of imagining that your intimate life is *not* important to you, I have a prediction: the rest of your life will inevitably become unworkable, and sooner than you imagine. Your goal is to have a life that works. Since leading from home is an indispensable central component of that workability, the Process must become a priority.

Let's look at the misconception connected to the second question, "How long will this take?" This question, too, signals to me that the person who poses it definitely would benefit from undertaking the Process. Built into this question is what I call a "destination mentality." This mentality is a little like the restless kids in the car who are constantly asking, "Are we there yet? Are we there yet?" They are so fixated on the destination that they lose sight of the reality that the whole point is the journey.

The journey is life itself, and it is sacred. The Process is ongoing. The point of what I have shared with you here is to help you make your marriage a shared journey, a journey that contains its own purpose for both you and your partner. We don't finish such a journey, as though it were a grocery list. We make it part of our deepest identity. If we ever fool ourselves into thinking that we're going to be done learning, done growing, done getting closer to a state of oneness with our partner, then we are setting ourselves up for a big fall. This is not something we do so we can get back to the task of running a business or building a career. The Process is something ongoing, something we build into the *center* of our business, our career, and everything else in our lives. If we think to ourselves, "Once we get to the vacation we've planned, then we can connect with each other, but right now there's a company to run," then we are sabotaging ourselves. If it's not happening right now, it's not happening. Being there for each other needs to happen on an ongoing basis.

Most people I work with require the help of a mentor to make that minute-by-minute commitment to the Process a daily reality. I suspect you will, too.

Up to this point, you have probably learned a lot of things from this book that feel like mental certainties to you. The question is, how do you make them certainties in your heart? We have a saying in my line of work: The eighteen inches from the head to the heart is the longest eighteen inches in the world. If you would like some support and encouragement as you travel those eighteen inches, I hope you will reach out to me by visiting me online at www.kairoslife.net.

CPSIA information can be obtained
at www.ICGtesting.com
Printed in the USA
BVHW041142051020
590317BV00010B/128

9 781977 228604